Karin Palshøj is a journalist for the Danish national television station, DR. Among other responsibilities, she covers royal events and state visits.

Gitte Redder is a veteran journalist and has covered stories for most Danish newspapers. She currently works with the Danish Union Labour Organisation, LO.

Zanne Jappe Mallett has worked extensively in the Danish–Australian community as an accredited translator/interpreter and did the much-praised voiceover for SBS television of the wedding between Crown Prince Frederik and Mary Donaldson.

CROWN PRINCESS OF DENMARK

KARIN PALSHØJ & GITTE REDDER

TRANSLATED BY ZANNE JAPPE MALLETT

ALLEN&UNWIN

The English language edition first published in 2005

Copyright © Karin Palshøj and Gitte Redder, Høst & Søns Forlag, Copenhagen 2004
First published by Høst & Søns Forlag represented by The Gyldendal Group Agency and
ICBS, Copenhagen, as *Mary – kronprinsesse af Danmark*
English language translation © Zanne Jappe Mallett, 2005

Allen & Unwin
83 Alexander Street
Crows Nest NSW 2065
Australia
Phone: (61 2) 8425 0100
Fax: (61 2) 9906 2218
Email: info@allenandunwin.com
Web: www.allenandunwin.com

National Library of Australia
Cataloguing-in-Publication entry:

Palshøj, Karin.
Mary, Crown Princess of Denmark.

        1st English ed.
        Bibliography.
        ISBN 1 74114 749 2.

1. Mary, Crown Princess of Denmark, 1972–. 2. Princesses – Denmark – Biography. I. Redder,
Gitte. II. Mallett, Zanne Jappe. III. Title.

948.906092

Edited by Karen Ward
Cover and text design by Nada Backovic Designs
Typesetting by Prowling Tiger Press
Printed in Australia by Ligare

10 9 8 7 6 5 4 3 2 1

Contents

Preface

Can you write a sober biography about a crown princess without prying? Can you draw a credible portrait without the subject being actively involved? Can you write a book about Crown Princess Mary at all, without being accused of wanting to either criticise or romanticise the royal family? We have made an honest attempt and it has been a fascinating experience to piece together a picture of the woman who in the coming years will make her mark on history as Crown Princess and, one day, as Queen of Denmark.

It has also been a difficult task because the royal family and the court have been protective of Mary and also exceedingly taciturn. But rather than indulging in speculation and then risk being accused of passing on rumours and innuendoes, we have chosen to stick to the facts and in this way let readers get to know the Crown Princess; her childhood, homeland and cultural roots.

Many family members and friends clammed up when journalists approached them. 'No thank you. We do not wish to talk about Mary,' was a refrain we heard time and time again. Mary is a very privileged person in that her network protects her to an incredible extent, both in Australia and in Denmark. Friends and family must have a tremendous respect for her and they show the same discretion that Mary does herself. We thank those who nonetheless chose to participate in drawing this portrait of Mary.

The question is, can Mary in the long run continue to be so inaccessible, even perhaps dismissive of the press and the public? A modern monarchy with a modern crown princess must have an open and respectful dialogue with the people, and in this regard, Mary, Frederik and the royal court have a lot to learn.

Writing about royalty is not always a highly regarded and respected occupation for journalists. Some take themselves rather seriously and think it is beneath their dignity to write about the royals. Some have looked askance and ridiculed us for spending time and energy on this book. We pity them. Mary will become the Danish people's Queen – our children's Queen – and it will be fundamentally exciting to see how she develops and matures in her new country.

Thank you to our understanding husbands, seven children and good friends for their inspiration and support throughout. The creation of this book has meant more spaghetti dinners and videos than are good in the long run.

And we wish Mary good luck.

Karin Palshøj and Gitte Redder
Copenhagen, May 2004

Chapter 1

A HAPPY GIRL

The Princess was born on a quiet, slightly cool day in late summer. It was Saturday 5 February 1972 in Hobart, the capital of Australia's island state, Tasmania. About as far away from Denmark as you can get.

John and Henrietta Donaldson had become parents for the fourth time. Henrietta was not yet 30, but during the last six years she had already become mother to two daughters and one son. Now the family welcomed their fourth child.

It was a little sister. The Donaldsons' own little dark-haired princess was born at the Queen Alexandra Hospital. Her parents announced the birth three days later with a notice in Hobart's newspaper, the *Mercury*.

Donaldson. – At QAH, to John and Etta, a daughter (Mary Elizabeth)

The same day, on the other side of the world, 16,202 kilometres from Hobart, it was a bitingly cold winter's day. An icy wind blew in over Denmark, and the temperature did not budge from zero. The Danes were still in mourning after having farewelled their popular and much-loved King Frederik three weeks earlier. Deeply moved, the Danish people had followed the ascension to the throne of Princess Margrethe as Denmark's new regent, Margrethe II. The Queen and Prince Henrik's eldest son, three-year-old Frederik, was playing with his one-year younger brother, Joachim, unaware of his destiny. One day, Frederik would become King of Denmark. But for now, he was a little boy growing up in a home where Mum was head of state, and Queen.

Of course, no one knew then that the two children on opposite sides of the world would meet by chance 32 years later as man and woman, and that this meeting would culminate in a lavish royal wedding and Australia's first ever crown princess.

Mary Elizabeth Donaldson could have been Scottish. Her parents, John Dalgleish Donaldson and Henrietta Clark Horne, were both from the little fishing village of Port Seton, east of Edinburgh in Scotland.

John and Henrietta were schoolfriends and became sweethearts as teenagers. Mary's grandfather, Peter Donaldson, was a well-liked fisherman in the little village. But a call from an Australian company turned the life and future of the Donaldson family upside down. At the end of the 1950s, an enticing offer tempted Peter away from the windswept and often harsh environment of the Scottish coast.

Crown Princess Mary explains how it came to be that the family settled in Tasmania. 'My grandfather was a very qualified skipper and was approached by the Flinders Island Trading Company of Tasmania. He had previously been offered jobs overseas, but this one provided exciting opportunities for the family. Initially only my grandfather travelled the great distance but finally, the family agreed it was a wonderful opportunity,' she says.

Mary's grandfather, Peter, and grandmother, Mary Elizabeth (after whom the Crown Princess is named) had two children in addition to John – another son, Peter, and a daughter, Roy. In 1959, grandmother Mary and the two youngest children followed Peter Donaldson and migrated to Tasmania. John Donaldson was the only one who stayed in Scotland.

'Except for my parents, the rest of my father's family joined my grandfather in Tasmania. My father remained in Edinburgh to finish his studies at the University of Edinburgh and after my father and mother married, they joined the rest of the family in Tasmania,' the Crown Princess explains.

In 1963, four years after the rest of the family had moved from Port Seton, John Donaldson attained his bachelor's degree with honours from the University of Edinburgh. John and Henrietta Donaldson were barely 21 years old when they were married in Chalmer's Memorial Church in Port Seton on 31 August 1963. And after only a few months of married life, the newlyweds could at last migrate to Tasmania in 1963 and join John's family.

In Tasmania, John Donaldson got a scholarship to continue his studies and before long the University of Tasmania had become the focal point of most of the Donaldson family's working life. In 1964, Henrietta Donaldson was employed as secretary to the university's vice-chancellor, while John started teaching mathematics and continued with his studies. In 1967 he wrote his PhD thesis on numerical analysis with the title 'Errors in the Numerical Integration of Analytic Functions', under the supervision of Professor David Elliott.

John Donaldson was closely associated with the University of Tasmania from 1964. He served on numerous committees and governing bodies – among these, ten years as dean of the science and technology faculty and for a period of time as head of the mathematics department.

His career also took him abroad. From 1970 to 1971, he was associated with Montreal University in Canada. In 1974 and 1975 he took the family to the USA, where he was first visiting professor at the University of Houston in Texas and then became involved with the American space organisation NASA's Johnson Space Center in Houston. But in spite of Scottish roots and a career with international possibilities, the Donaldson family chose Tasmania, and in 1975 the members of the family who had arrived last became Australian citizens. The fresh air, clean water and endless, pristine beaches and magnificent forests make the island a perfect place to give children a healthy childhood, and that was what John and Henrietta Donaldson chose.

Mary Donaldson grew up in the Hobart suburb of Taroona, just a few minutes' drive from the city. The red brick house on Morris Avenue lies well protected from curious eyes. From the road the garage is the most visible part of the house. Greenery screens a patio, which was built on top of the garage. The white letterbox with the black number 3 stands on a wrought-iron pole alongside the driveway, and the house today looks ostensibly the way it did when the Donaldson family lived there. Enormous pink rose bushes line the drive. They were Henrietta Donaldson's pride and joy.

Morris Avenue was a lively road in the middle of an attractive new settlement. In some families both parents went to work every day, in others the mothers stayed at home. After school and on the weekend, the road was full of children of all ages who played together. The neighbours in number 1, the Watson family, built their house at the same time as the Donaldsons. The Watsons' youngest son, Samuel, is four years younger than Mary and clearly remembers his neighbours' youngest daughter. 'We used to play together or play cricket in the backyard,' he says.

Mary grew up in a safe and happy family with Mum and Dad and three older siblings. Her brother, John Stuart, is eighteen months older than her. Patricia Anne is almost four years older and her eldest sister, Jane Alison, is about six years older than Mary.

The family had several cats. One of them was called Pushkin; a black cat with a white neck and white front paws. It refused to leave the area when John Donaldson moved, instead taking up residence with the Watsons.

'The Donaldsons were a very bright family,' Samuel recalls. 'Everyone ended up at the university.' Jane is a qualified pharmacist, Patricia is a nurse and John is a geologist from the University of Hobart.

Mary's sisters still live in Hobart. Jane works at a pharmacy in West Hobart, and Patricia is a nurse at the Royal Hobart Hospital. They are both married and have three children each. Like the rest of the family, they enjoy being active. In their spare time, they work as instructors at the Hobart Aquatic Centre.

Jane is married to Craig Stephens, who is a partner in an accounting firm. They have three children: Alexander, Erin and Kate. In January 2004, Patricia married Scott Bailey. They have a daughter, Molly. From a former marriage with Ken Woods, Patricia has two children, Michael and Maddison. Brother John has moved to Cairns in tropical far north Queensland, where he works as a mining engineer in the gold mining industry. John is married to Leanne and they have two daughters, Cherie and Michelle.

'The Donaldson family has close ties to each other. You can say that about many families, but for John and Mary's family, it was an extraordinarily close and loving relationship,' says Mary's sister-in-law, Leanne. With only about eighteen months between them, the two youngest – John and Mary – were very close. They always played together and when Mary started school, it was big brother John who was responsible for seeing her safely home.

'John looked after me when I was little, and I was part of everything he did,' Mary said in a JJ Films portrait program broadcast in Denmark in May 2004.

John's wife, Leanne, adds: 'John and Mary enjoy a special mutual understanding, which is possible because they are so close. A lot of John's friends used to visit his home in Morris Avenue, and John laughs when he recalls that often they came for Mary's company and not for his.'

Mary's paternal grandparents, Peter and Mary, lived in northern Tasmania, in the island's second biggest city, Launceston. The family maintained their Scottish roots and values and when the whole Donaldson clan with grandparents, uncles, aunts and cousins got together, there was always Scottish music and dancing.

Mary's mother, Henrietta – Etta – spoke with the softest Scottish accent. 'The children meant everything to her, she was a real lioness of a mother,' says former neighbour Samuel Watson.

Everyone in the family and many friends remember Etta's wonderful barbecues and family parties. 'Every Sunday evening the family got together at a barbecue in the childhood home, and the tradition has continued, even after the four children left home. On Sundays they'd always come home with their girlfriends and boyfriends and as they got married and had children, the Sunday barbecues remained regular events – the cousins played together and the grown-ups had a good time too. The family had fun and really enjoyed each other's company,' says Leanne Donaldson.

Today, John and Leanne live thousands of kilometres from Tasmania so they can no longer just drop in for the Sunday family get-togethers. On the other hand, Mary's sisters and their families can keep up the tradition because they still live in Hobart.

Etta Donaldson was not the type to worry about what others thought. She would often hang the washing out in the garden or feed the cats, dressed only in her dressing gown. It didn't worry her in the least. She was at the heart of Mary's free-and-easy and warm childhood home.

'Etta was a wonderful mother, very enthusiastic. Her family and children were absolutely the most important aspect of her life. Etta and John took part in all sorts of sports events and school functions; they were incredibly active parents. The children were always supported by their parents,' says Mary's uncle John Pugh. He is married to Mary's father's little sister, Roy, and the two families lived close to each other for 30 years.

Mary's father travelled quite a bit, recalls Samuel Watson. And when he was at home, John Donaldson made sure he kept in shape. As a young man at home in Scotland, John was captain of both the university rugby and cricket teams, and he continued to play for the local rugby team in Hobart when he and Etta moved to Tasmania. He maintained his interest in rugby, and at one stage in the 1980s he was a referee for Samuel Watson's rugby team.

John Donaldson was also mad about running. 'Find the steepest hill – and you'd find John,' says Samuel, and adds, 'and he hasn't changed.'

John Donaldson could also shout very loudly on occasion. Once when Samuel's big brother Christopher scratched some drawings in the duco of the Donaldsons' family car, John could be heard at a great distance. Suddenly, Samuel is again a mischievous little boy as he remembers John Donaldson's nickname among the boys in Morris Avenue. They called him 'Captain Haddock' – the name of the fiery captain in Hergé's *Tintin* comic strip – because of his full black beard and deep Scottish voice. The sound of Captain Haddock's vigorous voice on this one occasion is the episode that Samuel remembers best about John Donaldson; the family was loving, but also discreet and very private.

John Donaldson's own children also describe him as a strict father. Eldest daughter Jane remembers that her father was hardest on her while Mary, as the youngest, could get away with things that her big sister could not.

In a TV interview Mary confirms that as a teenager she was allowed much more freedom than her sisters had been given. The older girls had to adhere to set curfews, and they had to promise their parents to be home at a time when their friends were probably just getting into the partying, Mary has said.

In the same interview, John Donaldson admits that he was probably more of a disciplinarian than necessary. 'I think that most of my friends thought that I was very strict on the children. I presume I was. I did what I could to see that they did their homework so they would know that a secure existence was something they had to work at.'

The children in Morris Avenue played ball and went to the beach together. The local beach is Taroona Beach but Samuel Watson recalls that the kids from the street preferred Grange Beach, which lies even closer to Morris Avenue.

Mary's interest in horses and riding started at a young age. Together with her schoolfriend Kerry McQueen she rode in the park that is close to Morris Avenue. Her interest in animals was so great that as a child she dreamt of becoming a vet.

Perhaps inspired by her father, Mary started exercising even as a young girl. She jogged almost every afternoon. 'Of course I didn't see her so often after she had left home, but when she visited her parents, I saw her go jogging,' says Samuel Watson.

As a young child, Mary was looked after outside the home for the first time while the family was stationed in Texas from 1974. Here, the barely three-year-old Mary started preschool in the newly built Clear Lake Elementary School in Fairwind Road, Houston. The school has a tradition of bringing kindergarten children together with pupils from Year 5 to establish friendships across all ages. The big children wrote and read their own stories

Mary attending a gala performance the night
before the wedding, Copenhagen, May 2004

Five-year-old Mary

Henrietta Donaldson

Mary (right) playing hockey for Taroona High School

Mary and Frederik with Susan and John Donaldson at their
home in Sandy Bay, Hobart, January 2004

aloud for the smaller ones, and the little ones felt more comfortable at school knowing they had older buddies. So it was within this secure framework that Mary started her schooling.

Home again in Tasmania, Mary continued in kindergarten at Sandy Bay Infant School near the family home in Taroona. Here she was taught by Jane Kruup, who to this day clearly remembers the little girl.

'She still has the same lovely smile that she had then,' says Jane Kruup. 'Mary was the type of child who did what she was told, and she helped the other children. Everything one could wish for in a good student,' she adds.

Mary went to Sandy Bay Infant School with her brother, John, until 1978, when she started at Waimea Heights Primary School. The school had about 200 students, primarily from the local area of Sandy Bay, from kindergarten to Year 6. Students come from families that have high educational expectations of their children. The school is close to the university and is therefore a popular choice with parents who study or are employed there – as were Mary Donaldson's parents.

'Our students are articulate and individualistic people who have great intellectual and social potential. This potential is being developed to provide our country with responsible, informed, forward-thinking citizens and indeed future leaders,' the school's parent information book states.

Waimea Heights Primary School operates on the principle that from the time they begin school, students have certain rights and responsibilities. It is all part of the school's 'Code of Conduct'. The rights ensure that the children are not disturbed or harassed by others, and that they are treated with respect and in fairness at all times. But in turn the children have the responsibility to treat others with respect and not to trouble them in any way.

Mary's first teacher, Jane Kruup, is now working at Waimea Heights Primary School, and as a prelude to the school's fiftieth anniversary on 28 October 2003, the students sent an invitation to their former student Mary in Denmark. Mary didn't turn up for the jubilee, but the school received a thankyou card 'on behalf of the Crown Prince and Mary Donaldson,' says Jane Kruup with pride in her voice.

Mary attended high school at nearby Taroona High School, which is situated in a prime position on the banks of the River Derwent overlooking a sandy beach and rocky foreshore. The school has about 600 students from years 7 to 10 and the classes are named after colours. Mary Donaldson was in the azure blue class.

In addition to academic subjects, the school encourages students to be involved in sport and music, and Mary was happy to be part of it all.

'As a child I had piano lessons. At school, I played the clarinet and later progressed to the flute,' says Crown Princess Mary. Big brother John is a competent guitarist so the Donaldson home resounded with music.

With other children from Morris Avenue, Mary made the fifteen-minute walk to school each day. Taroona High School had a very good reputation and its students came from near and far, all dressed in their blue school uniforms.

One of those who came by bus from far away was Dan Jensen. He was in the same year as Mary, and in years 9 and 10 he took science and mathematics at the higher level with her.

'It is no secret that she is beautiful, but she is also very intelligent,' says Dan. 'She attended the most advanced classes – science, English, mathematics – and she was good at it all.

'Mary had "get up and go" – lots of energy. It was evident that she was happy at school. She liked to learn, liked to do things well. She was very good at sport. Especially basketball, but actually most sports – maybe with the exception of athletics. And she was wild about riding,' Dan Jensen recalls.

Mary belonged to a popular group at Taroona High School.

'She got on well with everybody, and she was absolutely among the most popular girls in the school. I cannot remember that she had a boyfriend while she was at Taroona, but there must have been many who were interested in her.'

Dan Jensen still lives in Tasmania where he works as a technical draftsman. He has only met Mary once since they went to school together.

After the connection between Mary and the Danish Crown Prince became public knowledge, Dan Jensen ran into one of their mutual classmates, who wasn't at all surprised that this had happened to the most beautiful girl in the class. 'Mary was the pick of the bunch,' as he put it.

Dan Jensen's father was born in Denmark, and he migrated to Tasmania in the 1960s. Dan was born and grew up in Tasmania, but he still has his roots in Denmark.

For him, his former schoolmate's new life and role is incredible. 'Just think that the girl I went to school with will one day become Queen of Denmark and rule over all my friends and my family in Denmark. It's a surreal thought. I believe Danish people will like Mary as their queen. She will adapt herself to becoming queen,' Dan Jensen adds.

Mary has several close girlfriends from her school days. Joanne Smith was a good friend with whom Mary shared her interest in horses. Another is Mandy Ellis. She still lives in Tasmania where she works as a teacher. Mandy was Mary's closest confidante when they went to school together and they have maintained a close relationship. In January 2003, when Mary returned to Hobart to follow Crown Prince Frederik, who was sailing in the Dragon class world championships, Mandy was one of the girlfriends who accompanied her through the media fray. Kate Wiseman was another good friend. Like Mary, at Taroona High she served on the Student Representative Council – a role that students take very seriously. Members are elected by their peers and have responsibility for a wide range of activities. Candidates define their values and aims for the school community and outline a proposed program of activities for fellow students. 'You have to be hardworking, you must be ready to give of your own leisure time for the school, and you must be interested in the community and the students,' says Oliver Hinns, who is one of the current members of the Student Representative Council at Taroona.

Mary was elected to the council and was even elected chairperson. Only one of Mary's teachers still teaches at Taroona High; the other staff members have moved on. But senior teacher Geoff Lockhart remembers Mary Donaldson as a studious pupil. 'My recollection of her is that she was a very clever student who was very popular with her schoolfriends, and that was why she was elected to the council,' says Geoff Lockhart. 'As a representative for your schoolfriends you learn responsibility, you learn to become a leader and you learn organisation, and I am sure that Mary Donaldson will need all these qualities in her new role in Denmark.'

The school's former principal, Robin Fox, adds, 'She must definitely have been leadership material. To be chairperson of the Student Council means that you enjoy both your schoolfriends' and your teachers' confidence.'

Mary was a happy, out-going and attractive girl, and of course she had boyfriends. One of them was Glenn Marriott, one year her senior, whom Mary met when she was fifteen years old. They were sweethearts for nearly three years.

'When Mary and I were going together, I always teased her by saying that one day she would find a real prince. We both laughed at that – but now I have been proven right,' he told the Danish weekly magazine *Billed-Bladet*. Glenn Marriott is today a tradesman and he lives near Canberra with his wife and young son.

Later on, Mary got a new boyfriend, Brent, with whom she spent seven years. They didn't live together, but had a close relationship. Today, more than six years after they broke up, they are still in close contact. 'We will always mean a lot to each other, because we've been through so much together. I believe he hasn't found the one and only yet, but he will one day. He is a very fine person,' Mary told the journalist Ninka (Anne Wolden-Raethinge) in an interview in the Danish daily *Politiken*.

On the winding road at the top of Mount Nelson, 340 metres above the city, lies Hobart College. It's an international school with 1500 students, many from Japan and a number of other Asian countries, and the college offers close to 200 different subjects.

Mary completed her Tasmanian Certificate of Education (higher school certificate) here in 1988. The college's current principal, Ron Nash, was also a teacher at Hobart College when Mary was one of the students. He trained her in basketball, where she played in a selective team, the Southern State Basketball Team.

'Here at Hobart College I have heard nothing other than she was a remarkable girl and an excellent student,' he says.

A wall in Hobart College's administration building is devoted to former students of the college, under the banner 'Where are they now?' Among the photo portraits on the wall are the founder of the business chain Chickenfeed, Rudi Sypkes; the head of the Anglican Church in Australia, Rev Dr Phillip Aspinall; the coach of the AFL team the Western Bulldogs, Rodney Eade; and Hobart's Lord Mayor, Rob Valentine. And there is a space set aside for the photo of another graduate – Denmark's Crown Princess Mary.

In 1989, after her final year exams, Mary joined the rest of the family and sought entrance to the University of Tasmania, where her father had by now been appointed dean of the science faculty.

One of Mary's good friends from the University of Tasmania is

Hamish Campbell, whom she met through mutual friends, and with whom she still keeps in close contact. Today, Hamish works as a stockbroker in an investment firm in Sydney. He is a couple of years older than Mary, and he studied economics at the university.

'Mary was a diligent student, and she read a lot, as do most academics. She also reads for pure pleasure. She is a very sociable person. She loves to meet new people and experience new ways of living life,' Hamish says.

There was a great sense of solidarity among the students at the University of Tasmania, according to Hamish. Tasmania only has a population of about half a million and less than half live in Hobart. Consequently, the university contributes a lot to the life of the city.

'We hung about at the university even when we didn't have classes. I didn't see much of Mary at uni because we belonged to different faculties. But Hobart is a small town and most of the students knew each other. We stuck together,' Hamish says.

Like many other former students from the university, Hamish has kept in contact with old student friends through the University of Tasmania Alumni. The organisation was established to maintain contact between students and their old university and between individual students.

The University of Tasmania has close ties to Indonesia and Malaysia, and there are local chapters of alumni in Sarawak, Sabah and Jakarta in addition to those in Singapore and Sydney. Mary has taken part in several of the organisation's functions, including one on 29 March 2001 at which the Sydney chapter was officially inaugurated. About 50 people associated with the university met at Sydney's Renaissance Hotel to taste Tasmanian wines and cheeses. Both Mary and Hamish were present on that occasion.

'We are all close. Most of us left Tasmania after graduation to follow our own careers, but at Christmas time, you can be sure that almost everyone I went to school with will show up, and then we catch up on what's happened over the year,' says Hamish. 'It's actually great – and a lovely thing about Tasmania: even if people move away all over the world, they will always have a soft spot for Tassie.'

Mary studied commerce and law at the university. Neither Mary nor Hamish Campbell was active in student organisations or politics. 'We concentrated on our studies,' Hamish says.

In her official biography, Mary says that in 1993 she was a finalist at the university in the moot court. That is a forum where law students practise presenting their arguments with weight and conviction.

In addition, sport and especially horses and horseriding were high on Mary's list of recreational activities during the limited time in between studies.

'It's like meditation. To go up to a horse and call its name and hear its greeting and its thrill at seeing you again – even if it's only to look for carrots and sugar, it greets you in its own way.' This is how Mary herself described her passion for horses in a Danish TV program.

Mary rode in the Southern Tasmania Adult Riding Club with, among others, the then club secretary, Brigitta Lowe. 'We rode together at the beginning of the 1990s. Mary was very good on a horse. She had her own big thoroughbred, Bold Interest, and they did very well in competitions,' Brigitta recalls.

Mary was especially good at showjumping, which she practised at the Tasmanian Show Jumping Association. Mary and Bold Interest jumped easily over 1 metre, and she got a first place and several other fine placings in competition events.

'Mary was relatively reserved when competing. She wasn't especially extroverted in the club, because she came there primarily to ride. Mary took her sport very seriously, and she didn't take part in the club's social life,' says Brigitta, adding that Mary always looked very fit and well trained.

Late in the afternoon of 27 May 1995, Mary's proud parents witnessed their youngest daughter being presented with her degree certificate at a ceremony at the University of Tasmania. Together with 23 other students in her year, Mary Donaldson could now call herself a bachelor of commerce and law.

'I finished my fifth and last year at the university in November 1994. The graduation ceremonies were generally held six months later and that's the reason I didn't get my degree conferred until the end of May 1995,' Mary explains.

And after that, Mary did what so many other young people who have finished higher education in Tasmania do. She moved away from the island. Next stop was Melbourne – the city of choice for young Tasmanians who want to get ahead and test themselves in furthering their careers. Melbourne is close by – about an hour by plane from Hobart or ten hours across Bass Strait by the *Spirit of Tasmania* ferries out of Devonport on the north coast of Tasmania. And Melbourne has the attractive and irresistible feel of an international city: Parisian charm with tree-lined boulevards, combined with many large companies and institutions that can satisfy young, ambitious people who are keen to tackle work challenges.

It was in Melbourne that Mary started her career in business with her first foray into the advertising industry. She became a trainee with the international advertising bureau chain DDB Needham working in various sections in order to learn the basic elements of marketing and communication. At the same time, she undertook courses – among them a course in marketing at the Australian School of Advertising. She also undertook a course in direct marketing at the Australian Direct Marketing Association. According to the college, this particular course aims at improving students' skills in advertising and enabling them to find out what is needed for an advertising campaign to work. More than 9000 students have completed this course, which carries recommendations from the advertising industry. Classes run three times a week over four months and can only be taken in conjunction with a job. And it isn't cheap. It can cost over $2000 to enrol.

Mary was quickly promoted to accounts executive in customer management at DDB Needham. Eighteen months later – in 1996 – Mary was employed by MOJO Partners as accounts manager. Her boss was Tim McColl Jones. Today he is a partner in the company, which has changed its name to Publicis MOJO.

'We have definitely not forgotten Mary Donaldson. On the contrary. Mary worked here for a couple of years. She was an accounts manager, which means that she worked with a team of colleagues who handled the same group of clients. Mary worked with clients like Hard Rock Café here in Melbourne and the Windsor Hotel, which belongs to the same group as Hard Rock Café. The Public Transport Corporation was another reasonably big client. She also worked with a finance company by the name of Esanda, part of ANZ Bank. Mary worked with me and with other creative people in developing advertising campaigns for these clients,' says McColl Jones.

He is excited when he talks about Mary's qualifications, as a colleague and a person. 'She possesses some typical Australian qualities. She is an open, outgoing person with a good sense of humour. She is a real outdoors type. Our good weather encourages active outdoor activities, and Mary was active. For example, she jogged a lot,' McColl Jones says.

Today, Publicis MOJO employs about 110 staff at its Melbourne branch. When Mary was there, the company had about 60 Melbourne staff. The office is on the fifth floor in Southbank Boulevard, in an area of the city where new high-rise blocks in steel and glass shoot up on every empty lot.

'Mary was an exceptionally professional, clever and intelligent person to work with,' says McColl Jones. 'She worked hard along with the rest of us in the branch and spent many hours at the office. We tried to get as much out of her as possible. Joking aside, ad agencies are workplaces that are full of young people with high energy. We have fun and we also work long and hard.'

The advertising industry attracts a wide range of people, both as employees and clients, and Mary was good at dealing with them all.

'She was very professional in her attitude to work. In our industry you are up against many different types of people – clients and creative people, who wherever they are in the world may be fantastic to work with, but they also have big egos. She was good at working with all types to create success-ful ad campaigns. If she had stayed with us, I'm sure she would have continued to have great success. But she is a girl who enjoys getting the most out of life and she was only in her mid-twenties when she was with us, so it's only natural that she wanted to progress.'

At MOJO Partners, Mary quickly became used to stepping out in front of large assemblies.

'She is steady and she behaves with tact and understanding. She thinks things over, and I'm sure she understands completely the responsibility that comes with her new role,' says Tim McColl Jones.

He doesn't remember Mary Donaldson as a fashion icon. 'She was not the type who talked about clothes. She was well dressed and a good-looking girl, but quite frankly, it didn't take much for her to look good. She didn't have to try very hard, because nature has given her good looks.'

At the time Mary was working in Melbourne, tragedy struck the close-knit Donaldson clan. Etta Donaldson had planned to take early retirement from her job at the University of Tasmania at the end of November 1997. But on Thursday 20 November 1997, she died suddenly from unexpected complications following a heart operation. She was just 55 years old. Her death was a great shock to family and friends. Strong family ties, both between Mary's siblings and their father John's siblings, were of great comfort to them all after the tragic death of Etta.

'Everyone in the family was devastated when Etta died. It was very traumatic, and the close family ties became even stronger, because all of a sudden everybody realised how much she had meant to the cohesion of the family,' says Mary's uncle John Pugh. Sister-in-law Leanne Donaldson, married to Mary's brother, John, adds, 'After Etta's sudden death, John senior and his four children spent some time together working through their grief. They had some heart-rending times together, crying and working their way through their sorrow over the loss of their mother, and I think it brought them close together.'

The family inserted a death notice in the *Mercury* that concluded with the words: 'Sailing 'cross the sea' – a reference to the Donaldson family's Scottish roots. Another death notice inserted by friends read, 'Oh, flower of Scotland, when will we see your like again.'

Several other commemorative words in the newspaper bear witness to the close family ties Henrietta had fostered. 'We know that the strong sense of family that Etta created will help you all through this difficult time,' one notice said.

The vice-chancellor of the university where Etta worked as executive secretary for so many years wrote a heartfelt tribute in the university publication *Unitas*:

'Etta's career in the University dates back to 1964, and hardly anyone presently in the University can remember the institution without her. She developed an impressive knowledge of the University, its staff and processes, which made her contribution to the work of the Vice-Chancellor's office invaluable ... Her serenity, courtesy and good nature were admired by all who came in contact with her. She helped maintain a positive image of the University.'

Mary

The university held a memorial service for Etta Donaldson with Scottish bagpipes playing to say goodbye to a valued colleague.

Henrietta Clark Donaldson's funeral was a private ceremony in the chapel at 71 Letitia Street in North Hobart on Saturday 22 November 1997.

Mary was just 25 years old, and she had already lost her mother – a tremendous sorrow for a young girl, and a pain and a loss that would leave its mark on her forever.

'My mother gave me the ability to see every human being as an important human being. She has given me my love of animals. They are so helpless, and we were both touched by their dependency on people's care and respect. These are some of the things my mother gave me. That each individual is important. I hope that when I have children I will be like my mother. I think that one's mother, in certain periods of one's life, is the most important person – one's greatest love,' said Mary to the Danish journalist Ninka in an interview in the Danish daily *Politiken*. In the same interview she talked about her deep sorrow after her mother's death. It was a sorrow that after some time she began to see as a gift. 'That's the strange thing about it, that through sorrow you learn so much. No matter how much you miss a person – in a way, you end up one day accepting that great loss and you find a way of seeing something positive in it. If you can do that you will really mature.'

In 1998, six months after her mother's death, Mary Donaldson left MOJO Partners.

'She came from Tasmania to Melbourne and, geographically, the next logical step was to go to Sydney. It is the country's largest city and supposedly internationally the most recognised city in Australia. Sydney has so many possibilities, and I believe it was what she was after when she moved on,' says Mary's former boss Tim McColl Jones.

There is no doubt that Mary had ambitions. In a TV program broadcast in Denmark a short time before the wedding, Mary revealed that she had counted on getting far. 'I saw myself as managing director of one of the international companies one day,' she said.

Her course was set for Sydney, but as a consequence of her mother's death, Mary took a round trip to Europe and America, and she settled temporarily in the country from which both her parents hailed. She went to Scotland.

'I still had family in Scotland,' Crown Princess Mary says. Like her mother, Mary places her family above everything else, and she used her stay in Scotland to spend time with her aunt Catherine Murray and her grandfather's sister, Margaret Cunningham.

Mary obtained a three-month contract with the advertising agency Rapp Collins in Edinburgh, a company that in Great Britain is recognised as the industry leader in direct marketing.

After months in Europe, Mary returned in 1998 home to Australia, specifically to Sydney, where she got in touch with her friend from student days, Hamish Campbell, who had settled there.

'When Mary got the job in Sydney, we renewed our contact. My sister had moved to New York, and Mary needed a place to live. So for a month or two, she used a room at my place while she was looking for her own place,' says Hamish.

'We spent a lot of time together at weekends. We went sailing together, we swam, cycled and played sport. We had many fun experiences together during the time she lived in Sydney. Mary is so full of energy. She likes trying new things, and she's so curious and without prejudices,' he says.

There is no doubt that Hamish Campbell admires his former fellow student. 'She is an outstanding human being with a big heart, a good head and a wonderful personality. And that's the reason no one can find anything bad to say about her. There are simply no skeletons in her closet,' says Hamish.

In a big city like Sydney, with more than 4 million inhabitants, it is of course also possible to maintain diverse interests, even those which normally demand space and green areas. Fuelled by her great love of horses, Mary could often be seen riding in Centennial Park in the eastern part of the city – among palm trees and lots of joggers, people on rollerblades or out on picnics.

In Sydney, Mary was offered a job as accounts director in the local branch of the international advertising agency Young & Rubicam.

'She behaves in a very honest way. She's very conscious of her career, and she is always absorbed by what she's doing, so there is congruity between her work and her attitudes. She puts her heart and soul into her work. And she could always vouch for her work,' says her friend Hamish Campbell.

One of her colleagues from Young & Rubicam was Trudi Ford, who worked in the accounts department.

'Mary was a really sweet girl. She was very out-going and enthusiastic. She was bubbly and charismatic, so it wasn't difficult to get on with her,' says Trudi. 'It was clear that she possessed managerial skills. She was strong willed and was determined to reach her goals. And she was not afraid to be herself in front of others.'

Mary advanced to the position of brand team leader when she moved up to her next job in the communication firm Love Communications at 38 Queen Street in the suburb of Woollahra.

One of the firm's commissions was a campaign aimed at convincing mainland Australians of Tasmania's many attractions as a holiday destination. For the client, Tourism Tasmania, it was important to target the campaign to potential tourists who were interested in nature, health and wellbeing and ecotourism. And without a doubt Mary would have been an excellent guide to her home state's exceptional qualities.

John Donaldson was alone for some years after Henrietta's death in 1997. However, in 1999, the British crime writer Susan Moody came to Jane Franklin Hall – an independent college under the auspices of the University of Tasmania – as a visiting fellow. That posting would turn the world upside down for both of them. John Donaldson and Susan Moody fell for each other.

At Jane Franklin Hall, visiting fellows stay for a time while they offer students and staff at the university the opportunity to engage with their area of expertise through lectures or seminars, discussion groups or workshops.

Susan Moody was born and grew up in Oxford, England. She published her first novel in 1984, and her novel *Penny Black* was the first in a series of seven about the amateur sleuth Penny Wanawake. She has also written several thrillers and romantic novels – some under the pen-names of Susan Madison or Susannah James. She has been chairperson of the Crime Writers' Association, and she spent two years as lecturer in creative writing at Her Majesty's Prison in Bedford. She has two grown-up children from her first marriage.

In 2001, John Donaldson accompanied Susan Moody to her home town of Oxford, where he took up a visiting professorship at the university. On John's sixtieth birthday, 5 September 2001, the couple married at Oxford. In 2003 he resigned from the University of Tasmania to concentrate on visiting lectureships in South Korea and at Aarhus University in Denmark.

The couple decided to establish their life together within a new framework. The house on Morris Avenue was sold and John and Susan moved to the fashionable Hobart suburb of Sandy Bay, where Mary had gone to primary school years before. Their new house is situated on a steep block with an imposing view over Hobart and the River Derwent in its hilly setting.

The couple chose the best of both worlds; spending six months of the year in Susan Moody's house in Chester Street in Oxford, and the other six months in Tasmania, in Sandy Bay.

And it is to the house in Sandy Bay that the four adult Donaldson children, their spouses and the grandchildren now come to visit John and Susan whenever the whole of the big Scottish-Tasmanian-Danish clan get together.

Mary at a university reunion, 2001

Mary riding in the grounds of Gråsten castle, July 2003

Mary and Frederik's first public kiss, Hobart, January 2003

Mary and Frederik visiting a museum in Aarhus, April 2004

Chapter 2

THE SECRET ROMANCE

Sydney was boiling over with excitement and in Olympic party mood on Saturday 16 September 2000. More than 10,000 athletes from 198 different nations had come to Sydney to compete for gold, silver and bronze medals at the new millennium's first Olympic Games. Furthermore, there were thousands of spectators and press contingents from all the continents of the world. Sydney was simply transformed into the centre of the world and the city's more than 4 million inhabitants had given themselves over to the festive mood.

The opening ceremony at the Olympic Stadium, about 20 kilometres from the centre of town, had impressed everybody. It had been a spectacular event. The identity of the person who would have the great honour of lighting the Olympic flame had been kept secret right to the last minute, and a thrill of recognition went through the 110,000 spectators at the stadium and the many millions of TV viewers, when the women's 400-metre sprint world champion, Cathy Freeman, appeared. Cathy lit the Olympic flame in a lavish stage show where cascades of water, light and fire were the central elements. The opening ceremony was simple, grand and moving, and many saw Cathy's contribution as a symbol of reconciliation between Indigenous and non-Indigenous Australians.

Heads of state from all over the world attended the opening ceremony, including the Danish Crown Prince Frederik and Prince Joachim. It was the Crown Prince's first ever visit 'Down Under', and after only twelve hours in Australia, he rose spontaneously and applauded when Denmark, as nation number 52, entered the Olympic Stadium fronted by Jesper Bank, the yachtsman and Soling class gold medal winner from Barcelona in 1992, as standard-bearer.

Together with Crown Prince Frederik's Lord Chamberlain, Per Thornit, and two security guards, the princes stayed at the fashionable Quay West hotel in Sydney's historic Rocks area. But their first 24 hours in the pulsating metropolis were not spent sleeping off jet lag in their hotel room. They arrived on Friday in time for the opening ceremony. On Saturday morning the princes watched their fellow Danes compete in the triathlon and in the afternoon they watched table tennis and then swimming. But the princes also had an arrangement to go out with some good friends on Saturday night. They didn't want to miss that.

So they met at the Regent Hotel in George Street. Several princes and princesses from European royal houses were staying here. The Spanish King Juan Carlos's nephew Bruno Gomez-Acebo had many years ago met the Australian Katya Tarnawski in London, and they had kept in contact ever since. Katya and her sister Beatrice had promised to show Bruno the best bars in town and the best places to dance, and Bruno said he would bring two friends along.

Beatrice says, 'I called my good friend Andrew Miles, with whom I studied design some years ago. I asked if he wanted to go out on the town with Bruno and some friends – I expected they would be Spanish athletes, who would be there for the Olympic Games. "Bring some nice girls," I said to Andrew, mainly to create some kind of balance between men and women because I took it for granted that Bruno's two friends were men.'

'It was a fantastic euphoric atmosphere when I met Bruno at the Regent Hotel. He introduced me to the Danish Crown Prince Frederik and Prince Joachim, the Norwegian Princess Märtha Louise and the Greek Prince Nikolaos. And they all stressed that they were looking forward to an informal evening. Frederik was in a good mood, almost like a playful puppy.'

Even though official Olympic cars with security guards were lined up outside the Regent Hotel to transport the distinguished guests around town, the princes preferred to take a couple of taxis. Bruno, Frederik and Beatrice hopped into the back seat of one taxi, and the bodyguard sat in front. Beatrice told the driver their destination was the Slip Inn. She only had to say it once; most Sydney taxi drivers know this popular venue well. Every weekend it is packed with people in a party mood, both locals and backpackers from all over the world.

Beatrice recalls that she had second thoughts about the meeting place. She knew that Andrew was waiting there with his flatmate Mary Donaldson and a couple of other acquaintances that she had never met. Was that good enough for a royal party? she asked herself, and she was almost panicking. On the other hand, she didn't want to disappoint Andrew, who was looking forward to the evening. She found it somewhat daunting to have to improvise when, unprepared and without warning, she had somehow become tour guide for a handful of European princes and princesses.

They arrived at the Slip Inn at nine that evening. Andrew was waiting inside with his flatmate Mary. Beatrice said hello to Mary and registered that she looked fresh and sporty. She was dressed in jeans and a sleeveless top with a metallic look in shimmering green and yellow colours. Beatrice introduced everybody. They all shook hands and began chatting while beer and margaritas were served. After drinks upstairs they all went downstairs where they were allocated three tables that the princes helped push together.

'By chance, Mary Donaldson was seated between the Crown Prince and me, poor girl. He was very open and interested in meeting everybody. At some stage, it was me who was taking the lead when the talk was about Australia,' Prince Joachim later said to the Danish magazine *Billed-Bladet*. Prince Joachim, who as a youngster in 1986–87 worked as a jackaroo near Wagga Wagga, had quite a good local knowledge, while Frederik at the time when he met Mary had only been in Sydney for 36 hours.

The party ordered pizzas, beer and wine, while the talk and the evening passed. More and more young people arrived at the popular meeting place. The bartenders and waitresses raced around serving the guests without knowing that they were a royal party. Only when the group was ready to pay and one of the guests handed them a Black American Express Card did the Slip Inn staff realise that they had distinguished guests.

When the bill had been paid, they all walked down hectic George Street to another trendy bar and restaurant, Establishment. Beatrice noticed that Frederik and Mary were conversing animatedly as they walked and when they arrived at Establishment, they stood close together, engrossed in a conversation and laughing together.

'I thought it looked interesting and when I left Establishment, they were still talking. The next morning I talked to Andrew to evaluate the evening, and we concluded that something was afoot between Mary and Frederik,' she says.

Thus started the fairytale romance – a tale in which a modern, independent and well-educated career woman, 28 years old and single, one evening met a modern, independent and highly educated man. During the first enchanted trysts in Sydney in September 2000, Mary would hardly have sensed that her life would change forever. They were two people just enjoying each other's company and the magic moments that always happen at the time of a budding romance. They got to know each other a little bit during those few evenings when the Crown Prince did not have official duties on the calendar.

At that time, Mary knew very little of the country which one day would become her new homeland.

'I knew it was the land of the Vikings, I had heard of Hans Christian Andersen and that the Opera House in Sydney was designed by a Danish architect,' Mary confessed to millions of TV viewers at the time of the engagement some three years later.

The numerous members of the Danish press who covered the Olympic Games did not discover the romance. The journalists only had eyes for the sports events and were oblivious to the dawning love affair, which would otherwise have made front-page news in Denmark. The Danish women's handball team fought their way to the quarterfinal, and after a nerve-racking match against France, they proceeded to a dramatic semifinal against South Korea. Both Crown Prince Frederik and Prince Joachim cheered the team when they went on to win gold.

In between sports events in Sydney and a short trip to Melbourne, Frederik visited Mary a few times. She lived in a charming two-storey 1920s terrace house in Porter Street – a quiet tree-lined street in Bondi Junction. Mary took over the lease on 1 March 2000. The rent was $780 a week, but was within reach when divided between Mary and two other housemates who shared the kitchen, lounge and two bathrooms. There was space to have barbecues in a small, charming front garden, and legendary Bondi Beach was less than ten minutes away by bike.

Number 20 Porter Street became a sanctuary for Mary and Frederik. Here they could hide from nosy journalists and merciless press photographers, and here they could relax and in their own time get to know each other. For Mary this sanctuary also meant that she got to know Frederik as if he were any young man. There were no bodyguards, no royal apartments full of regal furnishings, but a normal cosy house shared by people who helped each other and took turns to clean, cook and wash up.

When Frederik kissed Mary goodbye in Sydney at the end of the Olympic Games, they probably both sensed that this could be the beginning of something big and lifelong, if they dared give it a chance. But their love had to be allowed to develop away from the prying media and an inquisitive Danish nation.

Mary bound her closest girlfriends to secrecy, and at home in the cosy terrace house in Porter Street her flatmate Andrew Miles became her confidant. Andrew met Frederik several times before he left Sydney, and they became good friends. Andrew promised Mary not to reveal to anyone who her new boyfriend was. He kept that promise, and he has remained tight-lipped when talk turns to the royal romance that took off in his home. He wanted to shield Mary and Frederik's privacy, he said very politely but firmly when we asked him for an interview. And he added that he is very fond of both of them and respects them very much. That's the reason why he doesn't want to jeopardise a good friendship by speaking out of turn and perhaps disclosing something that belongs to their private lives.

Across the equator, the world's oceans and time zones, telephones and the Internet linked the young couple who were very much in love. It was very difficult for the young lovers to be without each other, and Mary's good friend Hamish Campbell says candidly that the telephone bills must have been staggering.

'Mary loved it when Frederik called, and that happened a lot. Almost daily. Their relationship developed on the phone. She spoke with him all the time, and there was no doubt that it was serious,' says Hamish.

As one of Mary's good friends, he often saw her at weekends. They went to parties together or went sailing. And Hamish smiles when he recalls a story about being out sailing with Mary when her mobile – which was always left on – rang. It was Frederik. Again.

'For us, her friends, it was just Mary's boyfriend who called and we didn't think much more about it. Mary introduced him as just "Frederik" and apart from the fact that he was Danish and that was different, the title of Crown Prince meant nothing. It was a normal relationship, and it wasn't as if anything special was made of it. But we loved to see Mary so excited. She was just so happy,' says Hamish.

After less than two weeks in Denmark, where the Crown Prince took part in the Danish Air Force's fiftieth anniversary at the Værløse airfield, Frederik flew back to Australia. Officially, he was with his good friend from his time in the Danish Navy's elite navy seals, the Frømandskorpset, Jeppe Handwerk and two bodyguards on a five-week round trip in the sunburnt continent. The trip was billed as a holiday, a chance to travel through the land he had fallen in love with during the Olympic Games, and which he now wanted to explore a bit more. That was the official explanation offered by the Danish court in answer to inquisitive questions from the tabloids.

Frederik was definitely in love and for the first time in his life as Crown Prince he was allowed to enjoy being in love without being besieged by journalists and press photographers. Once again, Porter Street became the backdrop for the royal romance. The young sweethearts would go for strolls in the area around Bondi Junction without much chance of their running into Danes who would have recognised Frederik.

Besides enjoying each other and being in love, Mary and Frederik also spent much time with Australian yachtsman and property manager Chris Meehan.

During the Sydney Olympic Games, the Danish competitor in the 470 dinghy class, Michaela Ward, introduced Frederik to her boyfriend, Chris. Both Chris and Frederik are keen yachtsmen and they quickly found they were on the same wavelength. Later they met again at a reception, and this time it was Frederik's turn to introduce Mary to Chris and Michaela. That was the start of a Danish–Australian double romance, which remained undetected by the Danish press.

Two Danish–Australian couples went sailing, cooked barbecues and found themselves really enjoying the time they spent together. It didn't take long for Chris Meehan to realise that Mary Donaldson had the potential to be employed in his company, Belle Property. As manager of the newly established real estate company, he needed a capable head of marketing, and Mary had exactly the qualifications he'd been looking for.

'At that time, Mary was working in another advertising agency. I told her we had a vacancy and asked her if she was interested. She said she was and she joined the management group of Belle Property at the end of 2000,' says Chris Meehan.

When Mary started at Belle Property, a company which in addition to selling top-class property and flats also publishes lifestyle and housing magazines, about a dozen people were employed there. The firm's office was near Kings Cross and hectic Darlinghurst Road, where cafes and ethnic restaurants line the footpaths. The area's bohemian lifestyle and notoriety as the haunt of streetwalkers and shady characters make it one of Sydney's busiest and best-known locales.

Belle Property quickly expanded and during the time Mary was working there, the number of employees grew to more than 100. Branches were soon established all over Australia.

'We fought to win a market share and everything happened quickly. We had a management team of five, and Mary was responsible for the marketing division. Every third month, the management team went on a weekend retreat to analyse the running of the company and establish new goals for Belle Property, and Mary was always a keen contributor. She worked very, very hard and didn't spare herself in the year she was with us. Building a new business means a big time commitment. Mary never complained, even though she often worked to ten or eleven in the evening before she went home. She was deeply professional, and if I could employ 25 of Mary's kind, I would do it without hesitation,' Chris says with a laugh.

'The clients appreciated Mary Donaldson the businesswoman because she had the ability to analyse clearly and had the courage to be direct. She had charisma, combined with great integrity and a serious side to her nature, and they were all wild about her,' he says.

When asked to identify Mary's strengths, Chris's answer comes promptly.

'Mary always presents well. In addition to being an extremely attractive woman, she always comes prepared, she's done her homework thoroughly, and because she's also intelligent and well spoken, she never makes blunders. At Belle Property, Mary could always give clear instructions, and she was able to cut through to the central issue extremely quickly. Many people waffle on without getting to the crux of a matter, but Mary would just come in and say "Right! We'll do this and this! Are we all in agreement? Okay, let's go!" She demonstrated leadership which was needed in the position she held, but not everybody can command such authority,' he says.

When Frederik visited Mary in Sydney, he also dropped in at Belle Property to meet up with her. But in the first year, the other Belle employees had no inkling that Mary's boyfriend was a true crown prince. Only Chris knew the secret.

'Frederik also spent a lot of time with some of my friends. I didn't think it was necessary to tell either my staff or my circle of acquaintances exactly who he was. He was just Frederik from Denmark, and that was all people needed to know. And I was sure that Frederik also enjoyed the freedom to be perceived as no different to anybody else.'

Chris Meehan also thinks that it was valuable for Mary and Frederik to have a private life like any other young couple for as long as it was at all possible.

'Of course, the Danish Consulate knew that the Crown Prince travelled to and fro, and they were kept informed when Frederik was in town. But apart from that, Frederik could move about as anybody else and be anonymous. No one knew who he was and he could do exactly as he wanted to. I believe it was important for him. And I don't think Mary needed the stress – she would have had to field inquisitive questions all the time if people had known who her boyfriend was. Quite simply, I didn't think that it was anybody else's business. So the staff knew nothing. Except for her closest friends and family, no one knew anything at all.'

While Frederik and Mary became more and more fond of each other, the Danish press still had no inkling about the real reason why the Crown Prince was in Australia again.

On 6 November, Frederik broke off his trip and returned to Denmark in haste. His beloved grandmother, Queen Ingrid, had become severely weakened after several weeks' illness.

All through Frederik's childhood and youth, the now 90-year-old Queen Ingrid, wife of King Frederik IX and mother of the current Danish monarch, Queen Margrethe II, had been a loving support and a good sparring partner when the Crown Prince had had existential crises over his role and duties. 'You can do what you must' had been Ingrid's stern rule of life, and she passed this on to her grandson, with whom she had a special and loving relationship because his temperament and attitude to life reminded her of his grandfather, Ingrid's husband, King Frederik. Frederik's grandfather, who was also called the 'Sailor King', was folksy and straightforward. He had been educated as a naval officer, complete with tattoos on his chest, and the Danes loved him because he behaved like a man; a human being, a father and a king – not a distant monarch, but King of the Danes.

Frederik didn't hide the fact that he was close to his grandmother, and when the call to Sydney came with the message that the doctors feared for Queen Ingrid's life, he left for home immediately, hoping that he would get there to say goodbye properly to one of the people who had meant most to him in his young life. One great love was growing in Frederik's life while he was about to lose another.

Frederik arrived home in time to see his grandmother. He drove direct from Copenhagen Airport early in the morning to Fredensborg castle to be with Queen Ingrid in the Chancellery house, where the two had a last confidential morning together.

Frederik paid another visit to Ingrid in the afternoon and also later that night.

Queen Ingrid died the next day. A chapter in the history of Denmark was over. Her daughters, Queen Margrethe, Princess Benedikte and Queen Anne-Marie (married to King Konstantin II of Greece), and the many grandchildren and great-grandchildren were grief-stricken. A week later they took part in a heart-rending funeral. Frederik was dressed in his naval gala uniform with his grandfather's Order of the Elephant and sabre, which he appreciated having received from his grandmother. His grandfather's legacy had been passed on.

Mary never met Queen Ingrid, but Frederik was filled with sorrow over the loss of his beloved grandmother, and through his heartfelt accounts, Mary was able to gain a picture of the strong-minded and playful woman who every summer invited her grandchildren to beautiful Gråsten castle in South Jutland (close to the Danish–German border) and who was the natural and warm centre of a large family.

The royal romance continued. Yet another handful of much-anticipated and still undetected trysts went ahead over the next year. Frederik undertook the tiring 24-hour flight to Australia via Bangkok, Singapore or Hong Kong at least five times during the secret year with Mary. And it seemed that he felt at home in the relaxed, unsnobbish Australian culture.

He got on especially well with Mary's friends, colleagues and flatmates. Everybody was on first-name terms with Frederik, who can talk knowledgeably about sport, but also take part in a robust discussion. Some of Mary's friends called the Crown Prince by the more idiomatic 'Fred' – shortening his name in typical Australian style. Like Mary herself, her circle of friends is free and easy, and even if they knew that Frederik was a crown prince they didn't discuss it.

'Like Frederik, Mary loves sport. They are both advocates of a sound mind in a sound body. He's a competent golf player; she loves to jog and run, to cycle and to sail. We often go sailing. She's an outdoor girl,' says Chris Meehan. As a close friend of both, he also points out that they share the same sense of humour.

'When they're together, they are very relaxed and quick to laugh. As a matter of fact, they laugh a lot. To be honest, I think it would be more difficult for a Danish girl to be a girlfriend of Frederik, because Danish girls have a lot of preconceptions about how to behave and be deferential to royalty. Mary hasn't – and I don't either, actually. She tells jokes, drinks a beer and puts him in his place, if needs be. She doesn't have any preconceptions of how she should behave in the company of a crown prince. She is just herself, and perhaps that's why they get on so well together,' he says.

Chris makes no secret of the fact that it was an advantage that they got to know each other in Australia and not in Denmark.

'I don't think that Mary knew at all what she was in for when she fell in love with Frederik. To be honest, I believe it was easier for her that they met in Sydney, and that she therefore had no inkling at all of what her future might involve. She had never set foot on Danish soil, never spent time in the imposing Danish royal castles. Frederik planned it very well. It was a slow learning process and in the beginning Mary did not understand the extent of the love affair and that it would change her life so radically. I believe that Frederik did the right thing by surrendering to the love affair and letting Mary do the same, without her knowing what was ahead. It actually took a long time before she really understood what was involved in being a member of the Danish royal family.'

Chris doesn't doubt that Frederik did a fantastic educational job by spending more than a year just enjoying his love affair with Mary while slowly introducing the independent, well-educated career woman to the price that was involved in marrying a crown prince and getting half the kingdom as a wedding present.

'He did all this very quietly and calmly – one step at a time. I believe it was the right way; that it was easier for Mary that she didn't know all that she now knows. She got to know and love Frederik as the man he is, not as Crown Prince Frederik. And that is a strength that their relationship will retain, and a balance that all relationships ought to have.'

Chris Meehan doesn't hold back when it comes to complimenting and characterising Mary. 'She has a wonderful sense of irony and humour, and she's a country girl … down to earth. Mary never loses touch with reality, and there is not a snobbish bone in her entire body. She's relaxed and toler-ant towards others. After she met Frederik, there were many outings to expensive restaurants, but she enjoys just as much to get into a pair of worn jeans and a T-shirt at home in her garden and put on a barbecue for her friends. For her, there's no difference. And I believe that in this respect, it's Mary's age and maturity that give her the strength to be herself,' he says.

After more than a year of secret romancing and many clandestine dates in Australia, the press corps of the royal-watching Danish weeklies set to work. Who was the Crown Prince hiding, and who would be first to disclose the identity and background of his girlfriend? In September 2001 the Danish weekly magazine *Se og Hør* revealed that Crown Prince Frederik's new girlfriend was Australian Belinda Stowell, who competed in sailing at the Sydney Olympics. The magazine printed a photo of the blonde sportswoman Stowell and reported that Frederik had succeeded in fooling everybody during the Olympics, when he disappeared from the face of the earth for several days to enjoy the company of Belinda.

Barring the report that the Crown Prince's girlfriend had Australian roots there was no truth to the *Se og Hør* story. When in October Frederik again flew to Sydney to enjoy both Mary's company and the Australian spring, it was to be the last time that the two would be allowed to stay anonymous. But they had had a year's head start on the Danish glossy magazine press, when *Billed-Bladet* in November 2001 lived up to its slogan 'Denmark's Royal weekly magazine', and published a front-page photo of the Crown Prince's real girlfriend, Mary Donaldson.

It was the journalist Anna Johannesen from *Billed-Bladet* who first broke the story and by doing so turned Mary's life upside down. Frederik had been in Sydney for two weeks and they'd enjoyed sailing with Chris Meehan in his yacht. When Mary turned up at work on Monday 12 November 2001, Frederik had already returned to Denmark on the Friday and the couple had by now known each other for fourteen months. After a long day at work, Mary left her office on the first floor and as she approached the stairs, Anna Johannesen was waiting for her with the all important question: was she Crown Prince Frederik's girlfriend?

'No comment,' was the reply from Mary Donaldson. A photographer snapped her in a tight red skirt and a black blouse. That picture landed on the front page of *Billed-Bladet* three days later. Now Mary was famous in Denmark and before too long, in Australia. Peace and anonymity were gone forever.

Mary's good friend Hamish laughs when he recalls the fuss once the romance with Frederik became public knowledge. During the time when the relationship between Mary and Frederik was still a secret, he met Frederik a few times and he considered him a nice, normal guy with some not-so-normal duties that he had learned to live with.

'When the news broke, Mary was shocked and not prepared for all the attention from the press. I don't believe that you can prepare yourself for that sort of thing. A short time after it became news I met her at Belle Property, and photographers chased us in our car. I thought it was great fun, but Mary wanted to escape at all costs, because she was such a private person. It was not easy for her in the beginning, when all of a sudden she was famous just because of her boyfriend. But now she's learned to tackle it and set her own boundaries,' says Hamish.

Chris Meehan concurs. He remembers that Mary got a shock when one November afternoon in 2001 she wanted to go outside to stretch her legs, until she saw a sea of press photographers outside her window. 'For a short period we had to employ bodyguards to protect Mary. We had something like 25 press photographers who almost camped on the steps outside Belle Property to get pictures of Mary, and journalists called incessantly to get comments from us. She was a bit shocked, and so were we. It was of course a big change and demanded some reorganisation,' says Chris.

About a month after *Billed-Bladet*'s disclosure, Mary terminated her lease on Porter Street, which was taken over by Andrew Miles, who still lives in the charming house. The lease expired on 16 December 2001. Mary went to Paris to teach English. But that was just a short stopover before Denmark and a new life with Frederik.

Frederik and Mary had known each other for fifteen months. Neither wanted to let the other one go and they were tired of having to make do with international telephone calls, emails and letters. They agreed that their love had to pass the big test, which included Mary's introduction to her new home-land and the duties which would accompany being married to a crown prince, herself becoming a crown princess and in the long term, queen.

'In a sense, we got to know each other in an old-fashioned way. We got to know each other through words, and we built a strong friendship and a good understanding through words,' Mary said in a DR1 TV program in Denmark.

Later, Mary said that in one of his letters Frederik quoted from the world-famous Danish philosopher, Søren Kierkegaard to convince her that she should take the plunge.

'Frederik wrote to me "To risk something is to lose one's foothold for a moment. Not to risk is to lose oneself." We had reached a point where we couldn't continue the relationship in the same way for much longer. We made the decision together that it would be easier for me to settle in Denmark than the other way around,' Mary said to DR1.

It is not surprising that Mary is a no-nonsense girl with both feet on the ground. Her parents were always straightforward. For both John and Etta Donaldson it was important to bring their children up to treat every-one as equals and not to discriminate, regardless of title or race. Equality and respect for others were fundamental values that were passed on to Mary by her parents and also strengthened during her childhood in Tasmania. In Tassie eyes no one advances by boasting of their position. The

Mary and Frederik's engagement is announced, Copenhagen, October 2003

Susan and John Donaldson, Mary and Frederik, Queen Margrethe and Prince Henrik
at the engagement announcement, Copenhagen, October 2003

Mary at her first official engagement, Fredensborg castle, October 2003

Mary and Frederik at Christiansborg palace in the week before their wedding,
May 2004

title of prince is therefore not important to John Donaldson. It is Frederik's nature and his daughter's love for him that matter.

'The most important thing for us is that Mary is happy. We are of course pleased that she has found someone she loves. But it would never occur to us to meddle in our daughter's love life. For us it is just about two people who are in love – whether it's a prince or a plumber she's fallen in love with,' Mary's father said to *Billed-Bladet*.

Being the very private and serious person Mary is, she was no doubt shocked over the way the Danish press exhibited her on front pages and posters day after day, week in and week out. Mary's story sold newspapers but she must have been uneasy about this. She had never sought fame, and now she had become Denmark's most talked about and photographed woman, without even opening her mouth.

Only Mary's closest girlfriends and Frederik knew the extent of her deliberations and whether there were misgivings before she made her final decision. Mary probably knew that any wrong move would be raked over by the press and proclaimed on the front pages of the newspapers and magazines. She would be watched over by bodyguards and hounded by paparazzi photographers. Although a very private person, Mary would have to come to terms with her new public life. It would demand adjustments.

There were pluses and minuses. On the plus side, Frederik was by her side and she was in an exciting country that offered her many privileges, great influence and the great challenge of becoming a crown princess. On the minus side, she could rarely spend time with her father, her siblings, and nephews and nieces, with whom she had close relationships. Her close girlfriends would be out of reach and her career would have to go. There would be less privacy and more exposure. There would be real pearls around her neck, glamorous party dresses and a social life bound by more protocol than an unaffected middle-class Australian woman could have been used to. It would be something of a culture shock for Mary until she found out how to cultivate her own simple and elegant style.

Understandably, Mary probably had her crises. To say anything else would be to imagine her as an inhumanly strong person. She had to change her main language to Danish and learn new pronunciations and turns of phrase. She wanted to preserve her own personality, but at the same time she had to acknowledge that she had to learn new customs, etiquette and modes of conduct. Danish authors, poets and iconic singers, such as Grundtvig, Adam Oehlenschläger, Steen Steensen Blicher, Kim Larsen and Tove Ditlevsen are people she had to get to know about, because they are all in their individual ways part of Danish cultural heritage, on which she now had to take a position. Mary had only a few months to get used to all this. From being an Australian, she was all of a sudden on her way to becoming a crown princess in a foreign land. She had to be sure to get to know the workings of Danish royalty and the Danish way of life, before she could finally say 'yes' to Frederick. She knew it had to be an informed yes, because it had to be durable. She knew very well that a yes to Frederik was also a yes to the Danish people. And as any other modern, independent and emancipated woman would, Mary probably contemplated the great costs of her new role. The responsibility, the duties, the press and the pressure.

As Mary explored her new country and language, she experienced the Danish summer for the first time. In Skagen at the tip of the Jutland peninsula she and Frederik paddled around in the sea and wandered through the sand dunes. All the while her love for Frederik grew. Everyone noticed it when they saw the two young lovers at a friend's wedding and at a rock concert with the Rolling Stones. Always hand in hand and smiling. They were also interested in each other's sports activities. Mary followed Frederik's Dragon class sailing. And when he took part in international competitions, such as the European championships in Ireland, Mary followed him with great interest – just as Frederik accompanied Mary to horse shows around Denmark.

Little by little, Mary built a good network of Danish girlfriends. They helped her furnish her flat at Langelinie in Copenhagen, a few minutes' walk from Amalienborg, where Crown Prince Frederik lived. Amalienborg, composed of four palaces set around a public square, is the main royal residence in Copenhagen.

Mary found out how aggressive the popular press can become when *Se og Hør* in May 2002 offered a reward of 10,000 Danish kroner (just over AUD $2000) to the reader who could snap the right picture of her with her boyfriend on Danish soil. Like the rest of the Danish press, *Se og Hør* had not been able to pull off a scoop when it came to the two lovers, so they resorted to rather dubious methods. But the reward offer was offensive to many Danes, and the rest of the press attacked the then chief editor of *Se og Hør*, Peter Salskov.

'Distasteful and wrong' was the opinion of the then chief editor of *BT*, Kristian Lund, about the reward campaign. The request for people to chase the Crown Prince's girlfriend all over the country had sinister overtones, according to Kristian Lund. 'There's a risk that we create a popular paparazzi culture, where everybody becomes an informer. We risk that people will provoke events in order to make money – that people will offend against even those closest to them for money,' said Kristian Lund in his own newspaper, adding that the method was 'an expression of rottenness in journalism.'

Whether Mary was alarmed by the heated debate, no one knows. But it was at any rate the beginning of the end of Peter Salskov's career as chief editor of *Se og Hør*. Revealing pictures of Mary did not pour in; instead for some weeks buyers boycotted the magazine in protest.

In May, the secretiveness stopped at last when Frederik and Mary allowed themselves to be seen together publicly in the town of Aarhus, where they frequented the trendy Cafe Casablanca, holding hands. And when Frederik participated in the Dragon Race of Jutland sailing regatta that same weekend, he took Mary to the idyllic Kalø Inlet. The photographers stood ready that same evening outside Amalienborg castle and when Frederik and Mary returned home in the dark blue royal Landrover, the first pictures of 'Pingo and Kanga', as many like to call them, were taken. Frederik was at the wheel, but it might just as easily have been Mary, who loves driving. Frederik's Navy Seal mates gave him his nickname from a penguin named 'Pingo' who featured in a popular Danish cartoon.

The magazine press took turns in guessing when the wedding would be. On the front page of *Se og Hør* in December 2002, Mary could read that she was getting married. 'Wedding May 24. To be married on Grandma's birthday. Chairs and dinner service ordered.' According to *Se og Hør*'s information 'several hundred gold chairs' had been ordered for 24 May, 'so that all the prominent guests can sit down, as is proper.' The magazine could also disclose that the Holmen's Church had been booked for 24 May.

The guesswork was not confirmed, but it secured the weeklies a nice circulation, week after week. Mary was silent, Frederik was silent, and the Danish royal court was silent. During Christmas 2002, Queen Margrethe was seen with Mary and Frederik at the Palads Cinema in Aarhus, where they watched *The Lord of the Rings: The Two Towers*. That the Queen was seen openly with Frederik's girlfriend was immediately interpreted as a seal of approval of Mary as a daughter-in-law.

Mary's grandmother on her father's side, who was one of the people Mary was closest to, died in the autumn of 2002, just when Mary had started her new job as a project consultant at the IT giant Microsoft just north of Copenhagen. Mary was crushed, but both her father and two sisters at home in Hobart advised her not to undertake the long tiring return trip to Tasmania to be at the funeral. Instead, Mary sent a heartfelt farewell letter in which she expressed her deep sorrow at losing her grandmother, after whom she was named, and with whom she had spent many happy holidays. The letter was read aloud at the funeral. In letters exchanged between the two, Mary had told her grandmother about her love for Frederik long before it became official. 'My grandmother was a proud human being and she could see something good in everyone. She had such a mild nature and a very warm heart. She thought of everybody in the family, and she did everything to hold the family together. I miss her. My grandmother taught me that what you give is what you get. I learned to be proud of who I am. Right up to the day she died, she was completely independent. She looked after herself and never complained,' Mary told Danish journalist Ninka in an interview in *Politiken*.

Grandmother Mary had wished for her ashes to be spread over the Tasman Sea off the breathtakingly beautiful Wineglass Bay on Tasmania's Freycinet Peninsula. The bay is also one of Mary's favourite places, nestled within Freycinet National Park with its spectacular granite peaks, coastal forest and pristine white sand beaches that delight all who visit. She spent many happy times there with her family over the years. Beside being famous for its many species of native orchids – one of Mary's favourite flowers – Freycinet National Park is renowned for its red granite peaks, The Hazards, and nearby Coles Bay is a mecca for recreational fishers in search of Tasmanian crayfish and the big game fish that can be found off the east coast.

Memories of Tasmania highlight what is most difficult for Mary in Denmark. It is not all the new things – but the loss of the old. 'It's a long, long way to Australia, so I miss my family and my friends very much. Also surfing. I miss some of the little things,' Mary said on the day of her engagement, 8 October 2003. By then she had lived in Denmark for eighteen months.

But Mary was not alone in the world. She had regular visits both from her Australian family and several of her good friends. Apart from John Donaldson and Susan Moody who visited Copenhagen several times, Mary's close girlfriend Amber Petty made the trip to Copenhagen to see her. They have known each other since Mary moved to Melbourne in the middle of the 1990s. Like Mary, Amber moved from Melbourne to Sydney after a couple of years to pursue new challenges, and the two women enjoyed a close friendship at the time Mary fell in love with Frederik. Like most of Mary's other girlfriends who out of concern and respect do not want to discuss their friendship with and impressions of Mary, Amber Petty also chose not to talk.

Another girlfriend from Melbourne, Michaela Ede, visited Mary in Copenhagen. With her husband, Sion Ede, she runs two exclusive fashion shops, 'Truffle Hunter', in Melbourne. Michaela and Mary have known each other for seven or eight years, and when Michaela opened her first boutiques a couple of years ago, Mary talked enthusiastically of Danish design. When Michaela and Sion came to Copenhagen in 2003, they not only visited Frederik and Mary at Amalienborg castle but they also spent time looking at the collections of Danish fashion designers, such as Naja Lauf, Bruuns Bazar and Day. These designs ended up in the Truffle Hunter shops, and they sold out very quickly.

'Mary knows Australian tastes, and Danish design is perfectly suited to Australian women. It's sophisticated, unique and relaxed. We sell out of Danish labels all the time,' Michaela said from her cosy shop in Drivers Lane. And Sion Ede revealed that he can speak a little Danish, because at the end of the 1990s, he lived for a year in Dragør and in Nørrebro, two suburbs of Copenhagen. He loves Denmark, and now there's an extra dimension to selling clothes with Danish brand names.

'Quality Danish designs sell like hot cakes here in Australia. It's not only because of Mary, but it helps. She wears clothes with such style. And that creates more interest,' says Sion.

Chris Meehan also paid several visits to Mary in Denmark with his fiancée, Michaela Ward. After Chris and Michaela have married and bought a villa at Rungsted, north of Copenhagen, they want to divide their life between Sydney and Copenhagen, and that means that the friendship between the two Australian–Danish couples will continue.

In addition to visits by family and friends, Mary made it a priority to maintain her lifeline to Australia. Her sisters in Hobart, her brother, John, in Queensland and friends in Sydney and Melbourne received regular emails and telephone calls from Mary in Denmark. At times, she confessed, learning Danish was a struggle.

In January 2003, the couple kissed each other for the first time in public – on the dock in Mary's home town of Hobart, where Frederik was sailing in the Dragon class world championships with his boat, *Nanoq*. The kiss became a sensation in Denmark. But if the couple so madly in love thought that after kissing each other in public they would be left in peace, they couldn't have been more wrong. The whole of Denmark reacted as if Mary had not only kissed Frederik, but the entire kingdom. They even wrote editorials about it and the kiss, which was on the cheek, was shown in slow motion on several Danish TV channels. That kiss was binding.

'This time it is quite true. It was officially sealed with a kiss in Tasmania. The Crown Prince was not going to get away with this. The timing was perfect; perhaps even a diplomatic stroke of genius from the Crown Prince. He was in Tasmania, on Mary Donaldson's home turf. He could not announce the engagement. Of course that had to happen at home in Denmark. But as a gesture, he could for the first time, here on Mary Donaldson's native soil, call her his girlfriend,' said *Jyllands-Posten* in its editorial of 21 January 2003.

'The next step was a harbour photo shoot, which he himself had arranged and where the young couple sealed their connection with the kiss. A future king cannot have such a photo lying around in the photo archives of the world if he intends choosing someone else as his queen one day. So what at first might have looked like an innocent summer's greeting from Tasmania was in reality a rehearsal for the engagement, which must be immediately impending,' predicted *Jyllands-Posten*.

But the Danes had to think again if they thought an engagement was just around the corner. Mary and Frederik wanted to set the tempo themselves for the decisive events in their lives and they did not return home in haste to declare a royal engagement just because of an innocent kiss. They stayed for another week in Tasmania after Frederik's Dragon sail race. It was clear that Mary enjoyed introducing Frederik to her family and that Frederik felt welcome in Mary's family, where no one stands on ceremony. There were relaxed barbecues in the garden and time to play on the swings with Mary's nieces and nephews. There was also time for bike trips to Mount Wellington and visits to bustling Salamanca Market, where the best of Tassie's clean, green produce and a wealth of Tasmanian arts and craft are all on offer.

Mary and Frederik also visited the Moorilla Estate winery outside Hobart, where they enjoyed lunch alone in the winery's gourmet restaurant. From here one can view both the vineyard and the wonderful museum of antiquities, an extensive private collection of artefacts from the world's ancient civilisations. Moorilla is an Aboriginal word meaning 'A rock by the water', and in fact right below the vineyard are cliffs with a wonderful view out over the River Derwent.

Moorilla CEO, Tim Goddard, invited Mary and Frederik on an impromptu tour of the estate and a private wine-tasting.

'Frederik clearly knows about wine, and we had a really good talk about the difference between French and Tasmanian wines. He is a wonderfully relaxed fellow and was very interested in hearing about our grapes and methods of cultivation. They spent a whole afternoon here, and finished the day with a cold Tasmanian beer,' he said.

The Crown Prince couple has since placed an order for Moorilla wine in Denmark, which makes Goddard proud. But like so many Tasmanians, he prefers to play down the new Danish–Tasmanian connection. However, the fact is that the Tasmanian winegrower has since been in touch with the royal couple and he says he's happy that Frederik, the son of a French winegrower, is also able to appreciate Tasmanian wine.

Back in Denmark after the visit to Tasmania, Mary engrossed herself in the job at Microsoft, and in her spare time she continued riding at a farm in Birkerød, north of Copenhagen, and received intensive lessons in Danish. In 2003 for the second year running, Frederik and Mary spent their summer holidays at Skagen on the Jutland peninsula. Once day they were ambling around in the charming harbour, which reminds her so much of Hobart. Among the raucous cries of the seagulls, the fresh sea breeze and the voices of fishermen who were landing the catch of the night, somebody heard Mary use the Danish word for trawler, *fiskekutter*.

'It's in the bag,' said the ironic headline in the daily tabloid *Ekstra Bladet*. When Mary can say *fiskekutter* in perfect Danish, then she will soon be ready.

Mary was starting to feel at home in Denmark.

Chapter 3

THE EXAM

It must have been the longest engagement in the history of Denmark. First came an intentional or unintentional slip of the tongue from Mary's possible future mother-in-law – a remark which was interpreted as the regent's consent to her son's engagement. Then came an official press announcement from the court that Her Majesty would give her consent at a meeting of the council of state two weeks later. And finally, the official engagement, when the impatient Danes no longer had to make do with looking at their new Crown Princess at a distance. Now they could see her waving and smiling in the flesh and hear her speak Danish.

It turned out to be two months of successful royal stage management and wooing of the Danish public at the end of summer. The anticipation was enormous.

For Mary, it was two months where she nervously rehearsed as if studying for an important exam. She knew the Danes would be assessing her suitability as a crown princess.

For Mary's Australian friend and former boss, Chris Meehan, who visited her in Denmark at that time, the huge amount of interest surrounding

Mary's engagement appeared somewhat out of proportion.

'It was quite fun to experience a royal engagement close-up … I visited Mary in the days before the engagement was announced, and we also looked at the questions from the press conference together. Of course, it created immense attention to become engaged to a royal, and no one can prepare for that, if you're not brought up in that milieu,' says Chris, who was impressed by Mary's tranquillity and style on the day of the official announcement of the engagement.

Months of intolerable suspense and guesswork were relieved on a hot summer's day – a Thursday in the early August 2003 at Queen Margrethe and Prince Henrik's castle in the vineyards near Cahors in the south of France. It is tradition for the Queen to invite the press to a meeting at the Château de Caïx, and this was the first time she said something publicly about her future daughter-in-law.

'We have met her, as you well know, and appreciate her,' said Queen Margrethe. When she was asked if she would get a sweet daughter-in-law, she answered in the affirmative: 'I think it will be fine.' At once, eager Danish journalists rang home to radio and TV stations. News bulletins broke into midday programs to proclaim that the Queen had confirmed that the Crown Prince in the near future would become engaged to his girl-friend of almost three years, Mary Donaldson.

The Danes and Danish press began a romantic feeding frenzy based on an unconfirmed future engagement. 'Mother-in-law tells tales,' said *Ekstra Bladet*'s posters the next day. Across eight columns, the daily newspaper *Berlingske Tidende* reported, 'Queen says yes to Mary' and *Jyllands-Posten* issued a special edition about Denmark's future Crown Princess. The main characters – the presumed shortly-to-be-engaged couple – were nowhere to be seen, and there was no kiss or hand-holding scene to satisfy the press.

At the daily newspaper *Politiken* they had fun with their tongue-in-cheek column, 'At Tænke Sig' (Fancy That), over all the royal fuss. With trademark satirical humour, the column lampooned the press for having pushed things a bit too far:

Excited studio host: Here is the TV news with a special edition. Her Majesty Queen Margrethe confirmed today that she does know that Crown Prince Frederik has a girlfriend. Let us first hear what the Queen said.

Queen Margrethe: Well, yes.

Excited studio host: This is what the Queen said yesterday at a press conference at Kaj's wine castle. Helle Bydum, you are standing at Kaj's now – what did the Queen really say?

Helle Bydum: What the Queen said, indirectly, was that she does know that the Crown Prince has a girlfriend.

Excited studio host: Thank you, Helle. And let us now hear the Queen's historic statement in slow motion!

Queen Margrethe: Weeeeeeeell, yeeeeeeeeeeeeeees!

Excited studio host: Merete Wiener Schnitzel, you are an expert royal watcher. What was it that we actually heard just now?

Merete Wiener Schnitzel: I don't really know. It sounds as if you have some problems with the tape machine!

Excited studio host: Thank you. I'm now told that our reporter Asbjørn Data is standing at Amalienborg palace square. Asbjørn, what's happening right now?

Asbjørn Data: Things are really happening here at the castle square. Half an hour ago, a bus passed by full of Japanese tourists, and a bit later it returned from the opposite direction, so there's no doubt that ...

Excited studio host: I'm sorry, I have to interrupt you there, Asbjørn, because we've just received an interview with a man who perhaps went to school with Mary Donaldson at Woolagoggagongg High School.

Man who may have gone to school with Mary Donaldson: Well, Mary was seven classes under me, but I remember clearly that she ate her lunch every day.

Excited studio host: This closes our extra TV news bulletin on the day when Queen Margrethe during a press conference at Kaj's wine castle said: 'Well, yes!'

'The Danes are wild about Mary', a Gallup opinion poll in *Berlingske Tidende* said only four days after Margrethe's statement in the south of France. The Danes actually took Mary at face value, and an overwhelming majority stated that Mary would be suitable to become queen some time in the future. According to the Gallup poll, nine out of ten Danes supported Frederik's choice of a commoner without blue blood in her veins. Danes welcomed the immigrant princess with warmth, a welcome that by no means could be taken for granted. Frederik's choice of girlfriend was Denmark's choice too.

And Frederik had done his work properly. In a JJ Films portrait program, Mary's father described how his youngest daughter's relationship with the Danish Crown Prince was announced in the family.

'While I was in Korea, I received a letter in which Frederik asked for Mary's hand. That was followed by a phone call. It pleased me enormously that he'd chosen to behave with such formality, and I had no desire to stand in the way of their happiness. I wrote back that I gave my permission and that I hoped that he would be a good husband to her,' said John Donaldson.

On Wednesday 24 September, the Queen's Lord Chamberlain, Ove Ullerup, finally issued a press release. 'The Royal house hereby informs that Her Majesty the Queen in the council of state, which is appointed to take place Wednesday 8 October 2003 at 10 a.m. at the royal residence at Amalienborg castle, intends to give her consent to His Royal Highness, the Crown Prince, marrying consultant, Miss Mary Elizabeth Donaldson.'

The Danish press went into yet another feeding frenzy – but this time they had confirmation of an engagement, albeit without the actual presence of the future bride and groom, who had escaped the hungry press to Italy. Newspapers, TV and radio repeated in increasingly inventive versions the same brief announcement that Denmark's future Queen and Frederik's bride was named Mary Donaldson. Mary dominated the front pages and the daily news posters without ever having said one word or called a press conference, and royal historians and experts were once again called into TV studios to evaluate the day's big event. The engagement ecstasy in the media continued apace. Among the many tributes was an editorial in the *Berlingske Tidende* that extolled Mary and described the future Crown Princess as 'a life insurance for Denmark's people's monarchy.'

The same day as the press release about the coming engagement was issued, Mary handed in her resignation as consultant at Microsoft.

The Danes had precisely two weeks to prepare themselves to meet their new Crown Princess. Danish and Australian flags were sold out in no time in the Copenhagen shops. The inhabitants of Copenhagen took time off from work and braved the autumn cold to wave their flags at the Amalienborg castle square. Nurseries and kindergartens planned outings and the shops in Copenhagen started decorating. The famous patisserie La Glace in the heart of Copenhagen baked engagement cakes after a traditional Tasmanian recipe and the cakes, with the taste of apple, cinnamon and walnut, sold – like the proverbial hot cakes.

Wednesday 8 October was the big day. The whole of Denmark was waiting to hear Mary speak. And it was to be a day when Mary and Frederik once again would demonstrate to all and sundry that they are in charge.

Firstly, they surprised the Danish press and public by announcing that they would marry on a Friday and not on a Saturday. No reason was given; that was the day they wanted.

Secondly, they chose to be married in the Copenhagen Cathedral, also known as the Church of Our Lady. Years of guesswork from the press had gone to waste. Everybody had counted on a Saturday wedding at the Holmen's Church, where Queen Margrethe and Prince Henrik were married in 1967.

Thirdly, the couple showed several times during the day that they did not intend to play the main characters in a soap opera directed by and for the pleasure of the press. The couple said no to revealing how Frederik proposed to Mary, and to kissing in front of the rolling cameras for a live TV broadcast. All the press got was a couple of loving kisses on the hand. That was the limit for the newly engaged couple, who wanted to retain a measure of privacy.

The program for the days of the engagement was hectic. The council of state was at ten o'clock, at which Mary's future mother-in-law, Queen Margrethe, officially gave her blessing of her new daughter-in-law to Prime Minister Anders Fogh Rasmussen. At eleven o'clock, Mary and Frederik met the government ministers and joined them in a champagne toast to celebrate the engagement. At twelve o'clock precisely, the newly engaged couple opened the doors to the balcony at Christian IX's palace at Amalienborg and waved to about 20,000 cheering Danes, Australians and other visitors to Copenhagen. The couple stepped out on the balcony four times. Hand in hand. In love. Smiling. Emotional. The Crown Prince had tears in his eyes. Only a man very much in love is that happy. Frederik, who for years had wrestled with the difficult role of crown prince, now experienced the homage of the Danes, an emphatic wave of happiness and acceptance of his future wife, which perhaps for the first time made him feel truly at home, happy and safe in his own royal house.

At 3.30 p.m., a press conference was held in the garden room at Fredensborg castle, with direct TV transmission. The garden room was

Fréderik sheds a tear as he watches his bride walk down the aisle,
Copenhagen, May 2004

John Donaldson walks his daughter, Mary, down the aisle, Copenhagen, May 2004

Mary and Frederik on their wedding day, Copenhagen, May 2004

Mary and Frederik receiving a blessing during their wedding ceremony,
Copenhagen, May 2004

crammed full of hundreds of journalists and press photographers. They had come from Australia, Germany, Spain, Great Britain, Norway, Sweden and of course from Denmark to cover the big event and to hear Mary speak Danish for the first time. The master of ceremonies and Lord Chamberlain was busy keeping the journalists behind the ropes and he guided proceedings with a firm hand.

It started with photographs being taken of the royal couple with their parents. In came Mary with her Frederik, her father, her stepmother and her parents-in-law. Never had Margrethe smiled so much and been so invisible. The press did not pay any attention to how touched Margrethe as mother-in-law was, because everybody was engrossed in Mary: tall, slender, smiling nervously, classically beautiful in a cream coloured dress. The flashlights clattered, the TV cameras rolled and Mary appeared for the first time at a press conference. The slightly perplexed parents and parents-in-law left the room and when the royal couple took their place on the sofa to start the press conference, you could hear a pin drop. It was Mary's turn on stage.

'Good afternoon, I'd like to say a few words before we start. I'm very happy to be in Denmark. Today is a very exciting day, and I'm sure you can understand that I'm a little bit nervous. I have read that I speak fluent Danish. Thank you! But it is unfortunately not quite right. It is important for me to speak Danish very well and I'm looking forward to being able to speak it fluently. If you ask questions in Danish, it would be a big help if you speak slowly. However, there will be some questions that I will feel much happier answering in English so therefore I will do so. Thank you.'

With those few words, incredible charm and a glint in her eye, Mary at once became beloved common property. Frederik and Mary showed they were head over heels in love, and when Frederik at the press conference was asked to describe Mary, his voice became heavy with love: 'It's hard to put words to something this lovely.'

Mary described Frederik thus: 'He's funny, intelligent, and warm. Everyone who meets him can feel that there's something special about him.' She answered all questions intelligently and had obviously prepared very thoroughly. At the same time she was wise enough not to espouse a ready-made program or to make declarations about how she intended carrying out her new role:

'I have an intense interest in many things, but what my biggest role is going to be I do not know. It requires a lot of discussion and a well thought out position, and it must be tackled strategically. So that is not something I can take up in this forum today, because it is something which will develop as I evolve in my new role.'

The media's examination of Mary lasted half an hour. The strain in the eyes of the newly engaged Mary disappeared minute by minute. She passed the exam with flying colours. With perceptiveness, integrity and wit in her replies.

Crown Prince Frederik's Lord Chamberlain, Per Thornit, who had been responsible for preparing Mary for her first press conference, gave Mary top marks for her debut. 'The engagement was a festive day, and the support from the thousands of people in the castle square surprised both of them. But it was a good introduction to the following press conference, which is an unreasonable thing, because it's almost viewed as an examination. You enter as a student, and there sit 280 examiners, but you don't know the syllabus. And then you're judged. It isn't reasonable, even though I believe that we hit the top mark. It was an intense experience for her.'

On the day of the engagement, the press got a glimpse of Mary's beautiful and simple engagement ring of two red rubies encircling a white diamond. Rubies stand for love and diamonds for strength, power and beauty. The engagement ring is worth a fortune, but precisely how much Frederik paid the Brazilian jeweller Mauricio Monteiro for the showpiece remains a secret between the Crown Prince and the jeweller. All we know is that four months before the engagement Frederik secretly visited the jeweller on a trip to São Paulo to discuss which precious stones and diamonds should adorn the engagement ring.

The day of the engagement was a triumph for Mary. The whole of Denmark saw this again at the gala party in the domed hall at Fredensborg castle. All eyes were trained on the future Crown Princess when, arm in arm with her fiancé, she arrived at her first royal gala dinner. In a simple and stylish dark blue silk dress which exposed one shoulder, with her hair elegantly swept up and with a two-strand pearl necklace, an enchantingly lovely woman of the world stepped out onto the polished floors.

Mary already looked like a real crown princess and by the following morning, everybody in the Danish media had surrendered. 'Mary is made of the material of which queens are made,' the welcome sounded in almost all the Danish newspapers.

At home in Australia, Mary's large circle of family and friends had excitedly followed her debut. The press conference at Fredensborg castle had been covered by Australian TV media, so now family and friends for the first time were given an impression of the radical change that was taking place in Mary's life.

When, a few months after the engagement, Mary flew home to Tasmania to be at her sister Patricia's wedding, everybody was anxious to get a first-hand account of life in the Danish royal house. But they were also anxious to see if Mary had changed in any way. The family could have saved themselves the worry, because according to Mary's sister-in-law, Leanne Donaldson, Mary's personality has not changed at all since becoming Crown Princess.

'She is the same as she always was. Completely down to earth and without airs of any kind. Mary played with her nieces and nephews and helped with all the household chores. Her new role has not gone to her head,' says Leanne.

According to Leanne, it is clear that Frederik feels at home in his large, unceremonious family of in-laws: 'He's a wonderful uncle for Mary's nieces and nephews. Frederik performs magic acts for the children, kicks a ball around and plays with them. My two daughters, five-year-old Michelle and ten-year-old Cherie are very enthusiastic about their uncle. Cherie especially adores him, because she can feel that Frederik is genuinely interested in her. He plays with the children with all his heart without affectation.'

Leanne was quite nervous the first time she met Frederik. 'My nerves were on edge, but I got over it quickly. Frederik is so easy to talk to, and in a short span of time I forgot that he was a prince and talked to him as if he was any good friend.'

Beforehand, Mary's brother, John, was also a bit worried about meeting Mary's new royal boyfriend. But the worry was quickly put to rest, says Leanne.

'John and Frederik get on very well. John thinks Frederik is tops and more importantly, we can see that Mary and Frederik are very fond of each other and very engrossed in each other. Frederik is perfect for Mary; that was John's conclusion after we had seen them together,' says Leanne.

And Mary's uncle in Tasmania, John Pugh, seconds these sentiments. He says he noticed no change in Mary. On the contrary, in her usual style she entertained the whole family in Tasmania about the engagement – without being blasé about it.

'Mary behaved exactly the way she always did. As a normal, relaxed person. And Frederik did too, and that's why we were so impressed by him. Not because he's a crown prince, but because he's good to Mary, has a sense of humour and is straightforward. He fits in with the Donaldson family naturally,' says John, and he stresses that Mary appears confident in her new role. 'Mary is happy in her new life. She is a strong and robust girl, so she will manage.'

Chapter 4

MARY AND THE MONARCHY

About a year before Mary fell in love with the Danish Crown Prince she voted, as did millions of Australians, in a historic referendum. On Saturday 6 November 1999, Australians went to the ballot boxes to vote on the proposal to convert Australia from a constitutional monarchy to a republic. The referendum asked Australians to decide whether or not to alter the constitution to replace Queen Elizabeth and her representative in Australia, the Governor-General, with a president appointed by parliament. In short, if Australians said yes, the monarchy would go.

Right up to the day of voting, there was drama and excitement about the possible outcome of the referendum, which had divided Australia. At times the debate between republicans and monarchists became strident. A poll taken a few days before the referendum showed that only 9 per cent of the voters were in favour of retaining Queen Elizabeth as a ceremonial head of state.

Australian social researcher Mark McCrindle is of the same age as Mary and has extensively researched the question of young Australians' attitudes to the monarchy. He offers this candid assessment of Mary's likely opinion on the issue of an Australian republic at the time of the referendum in 1999.

'Mary would probably have been a republican who voted to sever the ties with British royalty and no longer have the image of Queen Elizabeth on the Australian currency. Highly educated, with a progressive career, 27 years old and living in a dynamic, multicultural metropolis like Sydney, Mary would have been likely to want Australia to become a republic, detached from the British royalty. Statistically speaking, she's part of a generation that is republican with a proud feeling of being an Australian. Like most of her generation, she probably would have felt like dropping all that royal hysteria, and she would also have been likely to believe that Australia can stand on its own two feet as a nation.'

He hurriedly adds that even if Mary had voted for an Australian republic, it would not have meant that she opposed monarchy per se.

'Historically, Denmark and the monarchy have a natural solidarity, and that means the monarchy helps to give the Danes their identity and sense of community. The majority of Danes probably view the monarchy as relevant, while most Australians view the monarchy with indifference, as something remote and irrelevant. Many young people do not feel they have anything in common with Great Britain, Prince Charles or Buckingham palace. On the contrary, the young generally shake their heads over the British royalty, to whom they have an absolutely disrespectful attitude,' says McCrindle, who holds a university degree in psychology and a masters degree in sociology. Today he's head of his own social research agency in Sydney.

In spite of the extensive scepticism in Australia towards the British royalty, the referendum ended sensationally with a bit less than 55 per cent of Australians saying no to the proposal for a republic with a politically appointed president. The monarchists won the day. But Australians are still split over the issue. Many Australian republicans ultimately decided to vote for no change rather than have an indirectly elected president, appointed by a two-thirds majority of the parliament in Canberra.

Mark McCrindle explains the paradox: his research suggests that the majority of Australians are republicans, but they voted no to the new constitution on the basis of their ingrained mistrust of politicians.

'As Australians, we generally do not like authority. Nor do we like know-all politicians, who want to decide issues for us. We are very anti-authoritarian, perhaps because so many of us are descendants of convicts. We value our freedom and independence, and we do not under any circumstances like too many laws regulating our behaviour. In a way we are very different to Europeans … Australians want to decide for themselves, and the people do not want a president chosen by parliament.'

Although the Australian people said no to a republic in 1999, for Mark McCrindle there's no doubt that if or when Australians vote on the same question in a future referendum, it will be yes to a republic.

The former Premier of Tasmania, the late Jim Bacon, who was himself a supporter of a republic, said that a majority of people in Mary's home state voted to retain the monarchy.

'Queen Elizabeth does not play an active role and has no influence on the daily lives of Tasmanians. And yet, the majority would not dream of turning their backs on Buckingham palace. Many people here on the island feel there are ties to the Queen. Others think that the monarchy is pure anachronism, but they still accept the royal history,' he said.

Mark McCrindle is looking forward to seeing how Crown Princess Mary will manage her new role. For Australians there is now a spotlight on the glamorous side of the monarchy and Australians may, via Mary, attain a new knowledge of and greater respect for royalty. Now an Australian-born woman is a royal celebrity, a princess and a future Danish Queen.

'If Mary has success as Crown Princess and Queen, some Australians may change their views on the monarchy. But she will not fundamentally be able to change her contemporaries' attitude to the monarchy. They will continue to view it as something unnecessary in Australia,' McCrindle concludes.

The monarchy is under pressure from Mary's own generation. Not only in Australia, but also in the European democracies people who were born in the 1970s and later are very sceptical towards royalty. Princes and princesses who have inherited their power and privileges without necessarily having done anything to earn them are not popular among young people. Members of the younger generation have a much less respectful attitude towards authority, whether it be politicians or royals, and many young people regard the monarchy as a hopelessly outdated institution. Naturally there are those young people who romanticise royal celebrities and who are in awe of the glamour, glitter and ceremony surrounding royalty, but they appear to be in the minority.

That's why Mary, whether she likes it or not, will have to take on an almost unbearable responsibility for the image and survival of the Danish royal house. Can this young woman from the other side of the world help to modernise and thus strengthen the Danish monarchy? Does she realise that it would be easy for her to harm the royal house?

Even the smallest misstep on Mary's part could contribute to a royal scandal and disgrace. On the other hand, a fresh and flexible approach to the somewhat hidebound royal house could also turn Mary and the Danish monarchy into a cult.

The seeds to the renewal of the Danish monarchy may lie in the fact that a woman of Mary's background would be better able to reassess and revitalise old traditions, keeping the best and giving them a new appeal to young people. It is quite a leap from being a commoner and possible republican to Crown Princess, but Mary may also see the opportunity to create a new way of thinking about the monarchy, one which will accord to a greater extent with the attitudes of her own generation.

The curator at the Frederiksborg Museum in Hillerød (north of Copenhagen), historian and royal expert, Steffen Heiberg, says the role of the Crown Princess is one that is difficult to perform to everybody's satisfaction. But he doesn't hesitate in saying that Mary's greatest challenge will be to win the respect of her own 'republican' generation.

'Firstly Crown Princess Mary must be in agreement with the values and way of thinking of her own generation. If one is not in agreement with one's own generation, one has lost one's way. But in addition to being in harmony with her own generation, the renewal must also be consistent with the institution's dignity and its role in representing tradition and history. So it should not be rock music only, without any classical music – there must be room and respect for it all,' says Heiberg.

It's a natural expectation that the royal couple will renew the monarchy and set their own signature on it.

'With Crown Prince Frederik and Mary one could easily imagine a change of style, which is more in line with their own generation. One has to be a contemporary of one's own generation. It will be their judgment that will decide the strength of the monarchy, and its future significance,' Heiberg declares.

While the historian encourages Mary and Frederik to renew their thinking about their roles and the workings of the royal house to win respect from the younger generation, Lord Chamberlain, Per Thornit, the royal couple's closest adviser, is more sceptical.

To a direct question about how the royal couple should act to be in harmony with their own generation, his answer is straightforward. 'They should not be leading, but rather perhaps stay a bit behind.'

Since Queen Margrethe ascended the throne in January 1972, she has stepped up the ceremonial aspects of the monarchy year after year. The etiquette has not been modernised and made more casual and popular, says Steffen Heiberg. On the contrary, more uniforms and more unnecessary pomp and circumstance have been added. Everything is geared to maintain the picture of a regent and a royal house that is above the people – precisely what will make Crown Princess Mary's task harder.

'During the last decade, the royal house has become better at staging a series of events to demonstrate their standing and dignity. A stepping-up of ceremony has occurred. It may be to cover the fact that the royal house is becoming more and more populist, that the Queen is puffing up the ceremonial in order not to reveal that she herself married a Frenchman with – according to some people – the rather questionable title of Count. But pompous, self-interested staging creates new inconsistencies, because an old set of ceremonies must also harmonise with something modern and contemporary. Those contrasts are today very evident. A crown princess with a foreign ancestry will need to be clever to balance them,' says Heiberg.

Mary has an immense duty and responsibility but at the same time there should be room for her to be an independent woman who is sure to have her own ambitions about leaving her stamp on the royal house and views about how to use her newfound position of power to become a role model. Here, too, there are inbuilt contrasts which may be hard for her to handle.

In some ways, the monarchy has muzzled Mary, yet at the same time people are expecting her to be open and honest about what she finds right and wrong. Steffen Heiberg describes the tightrope that Mary must walk.

'Mary must be very clever and sense where the boundaries are for what she can allow herself to think and at the same time sense that the goal posts are moving all the time. The smallest slip may have conse-quences and mean that the minority's desire to abolish the monarchy all of a sudden will get more clout. It is hard to be a crown princess and a role model, because no one knows where the boundaries are, before they are crossed. And royals are not allowed to offend widespread conceptions and notions by presenting controversial views that provoke the majority of the population.'

Back in the 1980s Crown Prince Frederik's father, Prince Henrik, was said to have stated that one could rear children perfectly well with the help of a box on the ear – a sentiment that created a heated discussion among the Danes at the time. Steffen Heiberg thinks that if Crown Prince Frederik and Mary were to air similar views today it would harm the monarchy enormously.

'Frederik and Mary must not breach the conventions or in other ways be controversial, and that demands great insight and an understanding of what people are thinking and feeling, and of how to live,' stresses Heiberg.

If Mary breaches Danish norms, she will also harm the Danish respect for the monarchy. The balancing act will be difficult. For even though the monarchy is an immensely popular institution in Denmark and the major-ity of the population and the political parties support it, the modern monarchy has not yet found its place in a democracy, and that means it is not above attack, according to Heiberg's assessment. Contrary to the begin-ning of the last century, where the monarchy played a pivotal role politically, administratively and culturally, it is today almost politically inconsequential.

Just under 100 years ago, not only the Danes, but most Europeans began to look askance at the monarchy, because even if absolute monar-chies were abolished, the political powers of kings and princes clipped and democracies introduced, monarchies still played a central political role.

'The reputation of the monarchies took a dive after the First World War when millions of people lost their lives on the battlefield,' says Heiberg. 'The blame fell, among others, on the principalities and nobilities of Europe, because the military traditions of the aristocracy appeared absurd in the age of the machine gun. When princes and knights sent their men out to a certain death without a second thought, people lost respect for what they represented.

'The monarchy had no central role in the time between the world wars. But when the Germans occupied Denmark on 9 April 1940, the King became a symbol of Danish identity, and because the outer circumstances changed, the view of the monarchy changed too. From being a weak monarchy it became strong and that reputation has almost held till today. But it is also an expression of how quickly the popular backing of the monarchy can change,' Heiberg claims.

In line with the fact that the monarchy has become more and more peripheral, in effect a politically meaningless institution, the role and power of individuals within it has also become more peripheral. To remain relevant the monarchy as an institution must be able to qualify by virtue of some other perceived role, which has become the mystic, the traditional: history, ceremonies and the Order of the Elephant, which was established in the fifteenth century and is the highest order in Denmark. These send the signal that the monarchy is a venerable institution.

Mary must fit into a contemporary picture postcard image that is also part of a centuries-old institution. And as Crown Princess, her most distinguished duty will be to represent the royal house. To be a Crown Princess is to be a royal representative, but it also means playing a supporting role. Bar Queen Margrethe, who is the regent, Danish crown princesses and queens have always been second in importance to the prince or king.

'But representation is important to maintain power and there is a lot of prestige in being a good representative of and ambassador for the royal family. Bad representation gives bad prestige and publicity, while good representation earns respect. Everybody can draw his or her own parallels to Queen Ingrid [the wife of King Frederik IX and Frederik's grandmother], who was Crown Princess, and to the Prince Consort Henrik [Queen Margrethe's husband], who in a sense was also a crown princess. At any rate, formally Prince Henrik plays the same role as Mary is going to play when Crown Prince Frederik becomes King of Denmark one day in the future.'

Even if modern society and the political system can easily function very well without the monarchy, the monarchy can add something to society and give it an extra dimension, says Heiberg. For example, the monarchy can be used to foster political unity.

All Danes have experienced how Queen Margrethe and Crown Prince Frederik cleverly and professionally use the monarchy to unite the realm. They have made it a priority to signal that they are not only Queen and Crown Prince for the Danish people, but also for the people of the self-governing Danish territories of Greenland and the Faeroe Islands. In addition to being an enriching experience for the Crown Prince himself, Frederik's expedition with the Sirius patrol across Greenland's inland ice in 2000 also had immense significance for the Greenlanders' view of the monarchy. The many thousand kilometre long sledge trek undertaken by Frederik gave the monarchy an extra dimension and relevance for the Greenlanders. While Mary does not necessarily have to consider undertaking similar dangerous expeditions, she will perhaps herself be inspired by her husband's success. At any rate, she would be well advised to think in terms of valuing and promoting unity when she chooses the organisations and causes that will be the focus of her energy and vision.

No matter how popular the monarchy is in Denmark, the institution is fragile and absolutely human, with human frailties. Mary will be undertaking one of the main roles in the history of the Danish monarchy in precisely a period when the monarchy is in search of its own identity in a globalised world. Mary's own generation is at home in this era of instant communication which focuses on the present and has little sense of history. The world is borderless and constantly changing and inevitably, monarchies cannot remain untouched by change.

Both in Norway and in Sweden the monarchy is under heavy fire from the media as well as from a growing number of the public. The Norwegian Crown Prince Haakon's marriage to a commoner, Mette-Marit, who was a single mother and who has also admitted to experimenting with drugs in her youth, has brought attention to the monarchy's vulnerability.

Steffen Heiberg doubts that the monarchy can survive in Norway with a future queen who carries the baggage of youthful excesses. He points out that it is an interesting paradox: the norms of society have changed and today we all accept single mothers without blinking. But if the monarchy follows these same conventions, it will soon become an endangered species.

'It is an inexplicable paradox, but one that the royal family will have to tackle,' says Heiberg.

The Norwegian, Swedish and Danish royal families, democracies and cultures have over the years been so closely connected that a crisis for the Norwegian royal family is likely to also become a crisis for the Danish royal family and vice versa. The Danish royal family have suffered the unpleasant fallout from the uninformed debate that sprang up in the Norwegian press and public about Crown Princess Mette-Marit. The furore allowed the Danish media, who are otherwise royal-friendly, an excuse to break the taboos. The Norwegian journalist Liv Berit Tessem's book *Royal Watcher:*

Journalist in a Land of Fairytales, published in 2004, describes how public backing for the monarchy in Norway has been falling with lightning speed because of Crown Prince Haakon's and his sister Princess Märtha Louise's controversial choices of partners.

Liv Berit Tessem predicts that more pushy and aggressive media coverage of the royals may finally lead to the demise of the monarchy. Danish media no longer close their eyes to royal excesses. When stories and rumours, reliable or not, first come to light, they can be hard to handle. In Denmark especially the tabloid *Ekstra Bladet* and the weekly magazine *Se og Hør* have used the negative public opinion surrounding the Swedish and Norwegian royal crises to break taboos on negative reports of the Danish royals.

'It is very dangerous for the monarchy and it is an example of unexpected threats possibly emerging against the Danish monarchy, which on the surface looks strong, but in reality is very fragile. It may be that Mette-Marit is the biggest threat to the Danish monarchy for many centuries. When the media becomes tough in Norway and Sweden, a front line will open up against the Danish royal family from the north. When the Norwegian and Swedish press write about Prince Henrik's private life, the Danish press gets going,' Steffen Heiberg observes.

In that way there's a historically shared destiny between the three Nordic royal houses. If one royal house falls, it will no doubt be the beginning of the end for the others.

As late as in February 2004, the Swedish royalty was thrown into a tremendous credibility crisis when the Swedish King, Carl Gustaf, made comments about the Sultan of Brunei that were considered to be misinformed. The Swedish King was taken to task by the Prime Minister and afterwards publicly apologised.

An editorial in the Danish newspaper *Politiken* in February 2004 had fun with the royal crisis in Sweden.

'There is reason to be reminded … that even a constitutional monarchy has been reduced to a symbolic function; the monarch and their family represent the sum of a nation's history and culture to a diverse outside world. Expressed in modern management language, the regent is a valuable role model who precisely by being above everyday politics can play the part of a people's and a nation's moral guide.'

With that, *Politiken* indirectly described the most important task not only for Mary, but also for Frederik – that of being role models and moral guides for the nation. If they are to rise to the challenge, it won't do to have major contrasts between one's public behaviour and private life.

Till now, Crown Princess Mary has been the darling of the media, and she has by and large been spared any bad press. They have enthused over how well dressed she is, how beautiful, elegant, well educated and sporty. The press corps has almost seemed as deeply in love with Mary as the Crown Prince is himself. They have raised her to media stardom and proclaimed her a fashion icon.

Already the media has managed to manufacture a certain image and role for Mary as the carefree, horse-loving and fashionable Crown Princess. To marry into the monarchy is also, in a sense, to marry the press, and just as one has to set boundaries in a marriage there are also boundaries when it comes to media scrutiny.

'If Mary does not set these boundaries herself, all the newspapers and weeklies will gnaw away at her. Less-loving stories will appear. The royal family completely lacks media management skills and it is incomprehensible that they haven't engaged clever and professional journalists to tackle the press and help set these boundaries,' says Steffen Heiberg.

After the honeymoon comes the unromantic daily life – but the press will still be deeply dependent on printing new stories about Mary, just as Mary and the monarchy are dependent on press coverage in order that the monarchy can continue enjoying public backing and therefore legitimacy. The weeklies and the monarchy live off each other. In short, Mary has to make the press her friend and not her enemy. And this relationship demands that she give a bit of herself but also that she decide for herself the limits of what the press and the public should know.

In addition to being under intense media scrutiny, an amendment to the Danish constitution is something Mary must deal with in the coming years. Let's say Mary gives birth to a little daughter. Then a little brother is born. According to the law of succession, the little girl is heir to the throne. But only until a little boy arrives on the scene. Then it is the little brother who will become King, while the first-born girl has to make do with the title of Princess.

It is unthinkable that the Danes will accept that a girl is being rejected as a queen and heir to the throne purely on the basis of an outdated constitution. Women of Mary's generation – and Mary as a mother – will also find such a succession to the Danish throne incompatible with modern thinking on equality of the sexes.

It will be very exciting to see how Mary and Frederik will tackle an official debate about changes to the constitution, as parents to the future heirs to the throne. Tradition demands that the Danish royal family keep their mouths shut in any sensitive political debate. They must be politically neutral in order to be national symbols of unity. But can a mother and an emancipated, well-educated woman who has grown up in a family where equality between the sexes was a matter of course keep quiet in such a debate? Would Mary not be able to score points with her own generation, both men and women, by taking a position here? A future queen must be able to keep quiet, but she should also dare to speak – especially in matters where she herself is a central player. That's where she will be the next time the Danes go to a referendum about changes to their constitution.

To be Crown Princess and the future Danish Queen is to be observed in every respect. Mary must be a role model and will be pivotal in ensuring that the monarchy is perceived as being alive and relevant instead of fossilised and outdated. She must be the nation's moral guide and touchstone. She must be her King's wife and therefore not overshadow him, but at the same time she must also show that she is an emancipated and independent woman, a loving mother and a role model for other women. She must talk honestly and compassionately, and at the same time she must not become too intense, and she must not offend nor provoke anyone, just as it is a taboo to breach conventions. She must simply bring honour to the monarchy and not shame.

Mary is also a brand that is marketable. The Danish magazine and newspaper press learned that a long time ago. Big circulations and extra sales of weeklies and tabloids are guaranteed if the Crown Princess is on the cover. Mary and the monarchy sell. Ingenious and inventive people are already producing candles, cakes, cosmetics and perfumes that utilise Mary to increase turnover.

The Lord Chamberlain, Per Thornit, would like to stamp out such 'crudeness', and neither the royal couple nor the court are in favour of royal crowns, monograms and photographs being stuck on all and sundry to boost sales.

'It looks crude and it's vulgar, and we would like to maintain a certain dignity. We do not want to participate in an enormous commercial show, where pictures of the royal couple are affixed to all and sundry. There is hardly a product on the market that hasn't put in a request. Permission for monograms and photos is being requested on everything from porcelain to lollipops, from coffeepots to wine labels. No one gets permission. We will not take part in a commercial race,' Per Thornit stresses.

But the court is happy for people to celebrate royal events by placing photographs in windows and raising the flag on royal birthdays.

'When the staff in a nursing home ask permission to put the royal monograms on a layer cake to add to the royal wedding celebrations, they are of course allowed to do so. That sort of thing is nice, because it makes it more festive for everybody, without anyone making money on it. But we are determined to say no to the vulgar,' Per Thornit says.

One example of the marketability of the Mary factor is the Slip Inn in Sydney, where Frederik and Mary met for the first time during the Olympic Games in September 2000. Although the royal couple have not done anything at all since then to publicise the venue, the manager of the Slip Inn, Justin Tynan, does all he can to turn the royal romance into a marketing advantage. He appears in interviews in Australian and Danish newspapers, inviting tourists to the Slip Inn, where they might land a prince. The Crown Prince also features on the Slip Inn's menu and bar card. There's a cocktail named after him. For $12, visitors can try a drink made of lemon liqueur, mango liqueur and Malibu, stirred with soda water and passionfruit puree. Whether this concoction would be to the Crown Prince's taste is doubtful, but when this book's authors sampled it our first thought was: 'Poor Frederik'.

Justin Tynan doesn't hide the fact that he uses the royal couple's names to attract customers.

'Of course it creates enormous interest for the Slip Inn among Scandinavian tourists and Australians. It would be stupid of us not to take advantage of that interest, because we depend on our customers,' he says, and contemplates calling a pizza after Crown Prince Frederik.

We can only guess at the future for Mary and the Danish monarchy.

Many years may pass – perhaps decades – during which the royal couple will quietly enjoy family life and tend to their official duties and representations. As long as Queen Margrethe is alive and carries out her duties to perfection, the royal couple will live a more informal life, where they can direct their strengths and energies to tasks which are useful to society, and also enjoy sport and family life and children. Crown Prince Frederik will be a king in waiting. For Mary it will be a life as an apprentice – as a Dane and as a queen.

If the media continue to speculate on hitherto taboo aspects of the royal family's private lives, it may cause the popularity of the royals to fall dangerously, just as has happened in Norway and Great Britain. Looking at it from a purely media–political perspective, in such a situation it might be a prudent manoeuvre for Queen Margrethe to abdicate. Were Queen Margrethe to surmise that the monarchy and the royal house was suffering unnecessary harm, she could, by abdicating and leaving the throne to the Crown Prince and Princess, shift all the media attention to a happy couple who are still in love, and with whom the Danes are madly in love. In the history of Denmark, Queen Margrethe would be remembered as an exceptionally popular Queen who abdicated for the sake of the survival of the monarchy. In that case, King Frederik would inherit the throne and Mary would become queen, without having had many years as an apprentice.

Even if in Denmark there is no tradition for the regent to abdicate before time, traditions are there to be broken. In the past, the monarchy has been untouchable. That is no longer the case. The monarchy can be shaken and just as political parties and corporations monitor the goodwill of their clients and voters, the regent has to do the same. Queen Margrethe has worked very hard as monarch and regent over the last 32 years and it would be understandable if she chooses a course that others know as 'early retirement'. She might do worse than to abdicate and enjoy her retirement, leaving the throne to Frederik, who year in and year out has been chosen by popular vote as 'Dane of the Year'.

The Crown Princess is standing at the threshold of a new, challenging life. Whether it will lead to a happy ending for the Australian girl who fell in love with a Danish crown prince and had to take the monarchy into the bargain, only time will tell. Whereas her love for Frederik is genuine, her love of the monarchy is yet to be tested.

Chapter 5

PRINCESS SCHOOL

One of Denmark's oldest institutions seeks young, attractive woman for a newly created position.
- You will become famous and much admired.
- You will become a role model for your own generation.
- You must be ready to take your place in history.
- You must be a patron of welfare organisations.
- You will, with commitment, insight and empathy, represent a whole country.

Requirements:
- You must very quickly learn to speak, read and write Danish.
- You must know our history and culture and understand our sense of humour.
- You must give up your original citizenship and become a Danish citizen.

- You must give up your own religion and join the Evangelical–Lutheran faith.
- You must smile and be good at pressing people's hands and cutting ribbons.
- You will be followed and watched 24 hours a day, 365 days a year.
- You must give birth to an heir to the throne.

We offer:
- Free cars and several castles at your disposal.
- Servants at your disposal when you need them.
- Dresses created by the most outstanding designers, and valuable jewellery.
- Possibilities for exciting travel to exotic places.
- A chance to meet new people, whom others will only dream of.

Annual salary: 1,439,840 kroner [just over AUD $300,000]
Applications to:
Amalienborg
Copenhagen

This is what an advertisement for the job of Crown Princess could look like, were it not for the facts that the job cannot be applied for, it is not a career one can educate oneself for, and it is not a job that will ever be advertised.

Furthermore, there is another, intangible, specification. It takes love, specifically that between the Crown Prince and the woman who will marry him.

Mary got her new job as a gift the morning after her marriage to Crown Prince Frederik, and she was fully aware that she had not only married her prince, but the whole of his kingdom. She had acquired a life-long job along with her marriage.

'She has of course thought it over and she is ready for it. She is intelligent, so she knows what she is getting into,' says the Crown Prince couple's closest adviser and guide, the Lord Chamberlain, Per Thornit. The man who has been responsible for the education of Denmark's new Crown Princess received us in the middle of the hectic wedding preparations in a reception room at Christian VIII's palace at Amalienborg castle.

'For a person becoming a member of the Danish royal family and of the Danish society, the most important thing is to learn Danish. As a British ambassador who was in Denmark some years ago said, "The Danes are not a people, they are a tribe. And if you don't speak the language of the tribe, you don't become a member of the tribe." That has been the springboard for my teaching of Mary Donaldson, but also of Princess Alexandra [the former wife of Frederik's brother, Prince Joachim], for whom I was also responsible when she arrived in Denmark. All conditions for becoming a part of the Danish society lie in the language. And that's why we have concentrated so hard on the teaching of Danish. Mary Donaldson has had Danish lessons for two or three hours every day, because from the moment she has her Danish in place, she will be able to take over – then she can follow the topical news – politics, culture and everything else. That is the condition for her becoming self-sufficient. So she has been working very hard at it,' says Per Thornit.

Two teachers who also taught Danish to Princess Alexandra took on the task of teaching Mary. Having Masters of Arts in Danish and English made them especially suited to teach Danish to the English-speaking Princess. In addition to language lessons, Mary undertook other studies and essay writing. The tuition was to continue until Crown Princess Mary felt secure in her new language. Furthermore, Mary followed what was happening in Danish current affairs. She watched TV news and read newspapers. And according to the Lord Chamberlain, she is comfortable with the Danish humour and irony.

'We only speak Danish to her. I have also pointed out to her friends and acquaintances that they must speak Danish to her. It is so easy for us just to revert to English, but that is no good, because then she will get nowhere. So the Crown Prince speaks Danish to her and the staff in the house speak Danish, and of course I also speak Danish to her. And then we have an agreement that she says "stop" when she loses the thread. And then I must explain again, of course.'

The TV series *Matador* was an important part of the obligatory syllabus for Mary. This drama series, set in Denmark during World War II, not only depicts an important time in Denmark's history, the actors also speak very proper Danish. The characters of Maude, Red and Mads Skjern are Danish national treasures, and Crown Princess Mary got to know them thoroughly in connection with her language lessons.

'They were actors who understood how to speak Danish, so you can understand them. First Miss Donaldson and her tutors went over the texts and then they watched the shows. As well as the linguistics, it gave her a feeling for a period in Danish history which, although perhaps not absolutely historically correct, isn't that far removed from her own time in this country,' says Per Thornit.

Mary has a good ear for languages, and she progressed in leaps and bounds when she swotted over her Danish study book, her taskmaster told us.

In a TV interview on Denmark's DR1 Mary talked about learning Danish. 'It's hard to say what is most difficult. There are many difficulties in the Danish language. The pronunciation is hard. It takes a long time to learn Danish, because the Danes also speak English so well.'

And she changed to English when she described in the interview how she and Crown Prince Frederik communicate. 'We speak English to each other. It is a bit hard to change from English because that was how we met. We talk a bit to each other in Danish, when I have to practise … but mostly we speak English. And if I talk to someone from Denmark, of course I speak in Danish,' she said with a giggle.

In Denmark, the royal family and therefore also the new Crown Princess are subject to special rules determined in the so-called Royal Law of 1665.

The Royal Law says that, 'No Prince of Royal Blood who lives in the Kingdom and in our territory may marry, or leave the country, or take up service with foreign Lords, unless he has been given consent by the King.' That means that the regent has to agree to a marriage between a crown prince and a future crown princess.

For Crown Prince Frederik and Mary Donaldson that happened as mentioned earlier, at a council of state meeting at Amalienborg castle on Wednesday 8 October 2003, where the Queen gave her consent for the Crown Prince to marry. At the same time, the Queen presented the future wife of the heir to the throne and Denmark's future Crown Princess to the government. The engagement had formally become a reality.

A person who is entitled to succeed to the throne must obtain the consent of the council of state to the marriage in order to retain their entitlements, according to the law governing succession to the Danish throne. In other words, if the Crown Prince had chosen to marry without the consent of the council of state, he would have had to renounce his right to the throne and his future children would not have had any right to the throne.

The Crown Prince talked about his expectations of love in an interview with Trine Larsen from the Danish tabloid *Ekstra Bladet* in January 2002. At that time, Frederik had known Mary for a little less than eighteen months, and she had just given up her Australian career and moved to Europe to be closer to Frederik.

'I believe in – let's call it fate, and that I at some stage will hit the bulls-eye. I would rather wait and be quite sure. Under no circumstances will I compromise. But let time and love rule. I want to give it time. You must be able to feel it in here,' the Crown Prince added and pointed, according to *Ekstra Bladet*, to his heart. Nevertheless, Crown Prince Frederik thought that Cupid's arrow would strike him within the next couple of years – one, two or three years ahead. 'Yes, then I'll of course become engaged and marry. But I have a lot of things that I still want to experience,' he added.

The relationship between Mary and Frederik was in January 2002 still as unofficial as it could be, even if the weeklies had started writing eagerly about the dark-haired Australian. And the Crown Prince answered evasively when the question about the one and only came up.

'One can feel when it's right and complete. Of course I hope that will happen. But I'm not there yet – at the point where they say you can't breathe,' said the Crown Prince in the interview with *Ekstra Bladet*.

But even if Crown Prince Frederik would not admit it at the time, a timetable for Denmark's new Crown Princess was carefully being drawn up. Mary Donaldson had made the biggest decision of her life and was on her way to a new country, to a completely new life and a job that would eclipse anything she had previously undertaken.

To fulfil the formal conditions which are mentioned in our – albeit fictitious – job advertisement, a future crown princess must, among other things, be ready to relinquish her original citizenship.

Mary Donaldson was both a British and an Australian citizen when she met Crown Prince Frederik. On 21 January 2004, the then Danish integration minister and Danish Liberal Party member, Bertel Haarder, proposed a Bill for a 'Law about announcement of Danish citizenship for Mary Elizabeth Donaldson (No. 137)'. According to the law, Danish citizenship was accorded Mary Elizabeth Donaldson, born in Australia, with effect from 14 May 2004. At the time of her marriage on 14 May 2004, Mary Donaldson did not only become Crown Princess, she also became a Danish citizen.

At a time when the Danish liberal/conservative coalition government had tightened regulations regarding getting foreign spouses into Denmark, the first reading of the Bill went ahead quietly and with dignity. 'Yes', and 'congratulations', were the responses of most political spokespeople, although spokesman for citizenship from the Danish People's Party, Søren Krarup, added a political comment: 'There are likely to be some petty-minded souls – caught up in one or another ideology – who will be indignant over this Bill, because the future Crown Princess through this has been given preferential treatment.'

That prompted Kamal Qureshi, the citizenship spokesman for the Socialist People's Party, to say – in addition to congratulating the Crown Prince couple – 'We would like to see even more young people have the opportunity to return to Denmark with the person they love.'

In connection with the wedding, Mary also changed her religious denomination. The Royal Chaplain, Christian Thodberg, instructed Mary in preparation for the changeover from the Presbyterian church to the Evangelical–Lutheran church. Both churches have their roots in the Protestant tradition.

'It is very difficult to establish how the Presbyterian church is distinct from the Lutheran church, but the main thing is that there is a church communality between the two, in that they acknowledge each other, and there are no substantial discrepancies to learn about,' Christian Thodberg said to the newsagency Ritzau.

The Presbyterian church originated in Scotland and is characterised by the fact that it is not subordinate to bishops or kings, and that each individual parish is independent. And as the Crown Princess was already both christened and confirmed, her changeover to the Evangelical–Lutheran church could be dealt with in a few conversations with Christian Thodberg. The change of faith is not a legal requirement of the new Crown Princess, but rather a customary one.

In addition to Danish language lessons, Crown Princess Mary was also tutored in her new country's history and culture.

'She was reading Danish history very early on,' says Per Thornit. 'Palle Lauring's *The History of the Kingdom of Denmark* is brief, but it gives a very good insight into Danish history. And she has visited historical Rosenborg castle with her language tutors and there they went through Danish history. We are also going to take a trip to the national museum, where I intend to instruct her on the development of northern European cultural history,' says the Lord Chamberlain.

It was the Lord Chamberlain who planned what the Crown Princess was going to be introduced to as part of her education.

'She needs to join the community as soon as possible so I have planned visits around that. We started by visiting the Prime Minister, who discussed what a government does, and the political conditions in this country. Not so much about the current political climate, but more about the role of government and prime minister in general. Shortly thereafter we visited the Danish parliament and the Secretary General of the parliament discussed the Folketing [Danish parliament] and its place in our society. Then there were talks with some relatively young politicians, who told her why they have accepted the sacrifice of family life, and what drives them to go into

Mary's first visit to Greenland, June 2004

Mary and Frederik in Greenland, June 2004

Mary and Frederik outside their Fredensborg castle home

Mary during a Danish lesson

politics. She talked to young politicians from across the political spectrum. It was very exciting, and it gave her a lot of pleasure,' says Per Thornit. 'It is one thing to give her some brochures and books about the parliament and Denmark's constitution – and that's all right, but it is even better to talk to people directly,' Thornit adds.

It was on a Thursday late in February 2004 that Mary met with these young politicians. Among others, she spoke to the Conservative Charlotte Dyremose, the Liberal Rikke Hvilshøj, the Social Democrat Jeppe Kofod, and Kristian Thulesen Dahl from the Danish People's Party in the parliament.

'Mary was very absorbed and wanted to know how everything operates here, and especially how we as young politicians live our lives in relation to our families and where we live. She was very interested in our daily lives. I think it is fantastic that she showed such a great interest,' said Kristian Thulesen Dahl to the daily newspaper *BT* after her visit.

'We talked about how we view the world situation. And how it feels to be in the public spotlight. She was pleasant to talk to. We spoke mainly Danish and a little English in between. She really wants to practise her Danish,' said Charlotte Dyremose to the same newspaper.

The Crown Princess also paid a visit to the ministry she would have the most to do with in her official duties. 'The Foreign Ministry is very often the place where foreign travel will be planned – whether it is trade or cultural campaigns. She'll meet some people there and hear how these things are planned. And she will meet some of them again when she goes travelling,' says Per Thornit.

Mary was also introduced to the Ombudsman, and she visited the national bank.

As Crown Princess, Mary also became part of the Danish state budget in an indirect way. On 21 January 2004, Prime Minister Anders Fogh Rasmussen tabled a Bill for an 'Act to amend a law governing appanage for

Crown Prince Frederik (No. 134)'. An appanage is a royal allowance.

From the date of the wedding, the Crown Prince's appanage was increased from 3,706,000 Danish kroner (AUD $800,000) to 12,775,000 kroner (AUD $2,750,000). The increase was in light of the anticipated added expenses and representative duties which the Crown Prince would have after marrying, it says in the notes accompanying the Bill. At today's prices it corresponds to an increase from 4,176,945 kroner (AUD $900,000) to 14,398,401 kroner (AUD $3,100,000).

In this appanage is included a payment to the Crown Princess corresponding to the payment that her father-in-law, Prince Henrik, receives, amounting to 10 per cent of the appanage.

That revelation caused a debate. Should a modern woman have to 'make do' with receiving 'pocket money' from her husband, albeit a considerable amount, rather than being allocated a separate amount in the state budget?

'That is not good enough for Mary,' said Pernille Rosenkrantz-Theil, the republican spokesperson for Denmark's Unity Party. She demanded that Mary be paid half of Frederik's appanage, because a woman should not be dependent on her husband's moods and pocket money. 'In the Bill about a hefty increase in the Crown Prince's appanage, which the parliament will debate Thursday, there is no direct allocation to the Crown Princess. She won't get one krone herself for cutting ribbons, smashing champagne bottles against ships or accepting flowers from shy children. Instead, he gets 10 per cent extra, which he can use as pocket money for Mary,' said Pernille Rosenkrantz-Theil.

Crown Princess Mary is allowed for elsewhere in the state budget. She will be provided for if the marriage is dissolved as a result of the death of the Crown Prince. She will be assigned a residence befitting her rank with an annual basic amount of 6,387,500 kroner (AUD $1.37million).

The Crown Prince's appanage is calculated on the knowledge that the new royal couple must anticipate more representative duties and tasks than Margrethe and Henrik had while Margrethe was the Crown Princess. It means added staff costs. The Crown Prince couple will also have at their disposal Frederik VIII's palace at Amalienborg castle, and that again means added staff and housekeeping expenses.

But Crown Princess Mary is also expected to work for the money. The curator at the Frederiksborg Museum, the historian Steffen Heiberg, is the author of several historical books about the royal family and, according to him, the Crown Princess's duties are first and foremost representative.

'The representative role has always been there … she will be representing the royal family, which represents the state – for example when travelling abroad. So on that point, she steps into a tradition which has always been there, and then there's the usual cutting of ribbons, and she will possibly also become patron for quite a few organisations – scout movements and that sort of thing,' says Steffen Heiberg.

'But she must also make a mark as a person in her own right. For Queen Ingrid, South Jutland became the cause she made her mark on. She became a crown princess fifteen years after reunification [part of South Jutland was reinstated as a part of Denmark in 1920; Germany had occupied it since 1864], so it was of course an obvious cause. I don't know if it is an obvious cause today, but it would be wise for Mary to find something that could mark her for the Danish people in a positive way,' he adds.

Mary will at any rate take on a number of patronages as a part of her official duties. From the date of the engagement, requests to the future Crown Princess poured in, says Lord Chamberlain Per Thornit. For several years, Thornit also managed Prince Joachim and Princess Alexandra's courts, but in connection with Frederik and Mary's engagement he took over the post as Lord Chamberlain for the Crown Prince couple.

'We get quite a number of requests, but we won't consider anything until after the wedding. She must be allowed to think it over herself. What does she want to aim for, what is she interested in? She must be allowed to think it over in peace. It would be very easy for me to say "That's a very good idea," and she may see that as manipulation, when she thinks it over later on. She must be allowed to be part of it, so she knows what she is doing.'

All members of the royal family have organisations to which they feel especially attached in the form of patronages. At her wedding to Prince Joachim on 18 November 1995, Alexandra became a princess and since then she has undertaken duties professionally and with dedication in connection with the patronage of various associations and institutions like the Danish UNICEF Committee, the Danish Institute for the Blind, the North Sea Museum, Red Cross for Youth, Mothers in Crisis of 1983, the Danish Garden Society, Denmark Radio's Girls' Choir and many more.

Crown Princess Mary's friends have clear expectations of how she will handle the job of being a patron. Her university colleague and friend Hamish Campbell is certain: 'She will be really committed. As she won't be allowed to have a normal job, she will make sure that she has something meaningful to do – she is not the type to just sit around doing nothing. She will apply herself to the task with great commitment,' he says.

Hamish is in no doubt which areas are close to Mary's heart. 'She will probably want to support something humanitarian, and she will do it well. She will really apply herself to humanitarian work and work for the benefit of children. And animals, of course. Mary loves animals – she has done since she was a little girl,' he adds.

On their home page, the royal family describes what a patron's role is. 'When a member of the royal family takes on a patronage, it means that they commit themselves to favour the relevant association, institution, cause or organisation. This can be done in different ways, but generally it means that the particular royal supports the patronage by contributing to raising the profile of the particular group and, through their work, inspiring other people who also wish to contribute and support it in various ways.'

Royal patronage can take several forms. Often, the patron will make annual visits and also be present when the association or organisation arranges a special event. But it could also be that the patron regularly participates in meetings. Many of the humanitarian organisations have been given a promise of permanent patronage, while exhibitions, conferences and the like may only have a promise of patronage for a single event.

Mary's last Australian employer, general manager of the real estate chain Belle Property, Chris Meehan, is, as mentioned before, one of Mary and Frederik's close friends. He knew Mary as an 'ordinary' staff member and with this background he is well placed to evaluate how she will be able to draw on her business experience in her new role in Denmark.

'She was with us at a time in our company when everything was moving very quickly and she had to make a lot of decisions within very tight time frames. She is very good at that. She could familiarise herself with any situation, or she would be given a briefing about a subject and she could condense it all very quickly. She is very good at assessing a situation. And that will come in handy for her. Working with us, she had to relate both to the young girl who was transcribing the text and to the high-profile client – and she managed that very well. So she can manage the whole spectrum, and I believe there will be a lot of that in her new job.' He adds, 'I know this from Frederik – he is able to do the same. One minute he is talking with a head of state, the next with a bartender. And he feels comfortable in both situations.'

An important part of the Crown Princess's education is to learn how to behave in a dignified manner when she represents the royal family. Per Thornit outlines the demands involved.

'There are some ground rules for planning how a royal person attends official engagements and all that goes with them … I receive a program and I go through it very thoroughly with her. Whom she is meeting, whom she is speaking to and who are they? The rest takes care of itself. If you are involved, curious and engaged in what you are there to see, it is not so very difficult,' he says. 'But there is one thing I won't do this time. Princess Alexandra wanted to know *everything* about an engagement before she attended and that meant that her level of information was very high. When she attended it, she asked questions at a very high level, which many people could not answer. She would then return and say that we had prepared too much. If preparation had been at a slightly lower level, it would have been easier, you could react with ordinary spontaneous curiosity – ask a question and get an answer. Princess Alexandra wanted to do it as well as possible, and that is why we made rather too much of the background material,' Per Thornit admits.

While Denmark at the end of September 2003 buzzed with euphoria over the coming engagement, an article in the *Mercury* in Hobart caused a sensation in Australia. Under the headline 'Mary's royal babies pledge' the newspaper's correspondent in Copenhagen wrote that Mary – as one of the preparations for the wedding – had agreed to give up the custody of any children the couple may have, should the royal couple split up.

'Agreeing to her children remaining Danish and being brought up in the Royal family is only one of the major changes the future Queen Mary will find in her life,' the *Mercury* correspondent wrote on 26 September 2003. There is a logical, historical explanation for this, says museum curator Steffen Heiberg. 'In terms of the history, a princely child belongs to the state. The Australian media assumes that we're talking about a normal family, but in this country, the king or the monarch has traditionally had legal authority over members of the royal family. It is the monarch who decides what will happen to them should they commit breaches of the law. The latest example is when Christian X [King of Denmark from 1912 to 1947] expelled Princess Helena, who was married to the King's brother Harald, for unpatriotic behaviour after the occupation [by Germany in World War II],' says Heiberg.

But he adds that Mary, according to contemporary interpretation, will be subject to common Danish laws.

And Crown Prince Frederik's Lord Chamberlain, Per Thornit, dismisses the reports about Crown Princess Mary having to renounce her rights to any children in the case of a divorce. 'That is not right. Danish legal regulations and practice is what would apply in situations like that. No agreement has been made in that regard – and it won't be either,' the Lord Chamberlain adds.

Chief Clerk in the Cabinet Secretariat, Henrik Gram, who assists the Queen in carrying out her duties as head of state, among other things, expanded on this topic in the tabloid *BT*. 'Mary Donaldson is completely equal to Crown Prince Frederik. The custody laws also apply to the royals. There is no difference. The starting point in the case of a divorce is that the partners have joint custody. But if this causes problems because there is disagreement, a decision may be made so that custody is transferred to only one of the parties. In the end, only the courts can decide this,' says Gram.

But in practice, there would not be much that Mary could do, if she and the Crown Prince should choose to split and they could not agree on the conditions of the divorce.

'You cannot sue a member of the royal family. They can't sue each other either, so Mary would not be able to go to a Danish court and take legal action against Frederik unless the courts give her special permission,' said Professor Ditlev Tamm in *BT* in March 2004.

There are more down-to-earth, everyday restrictions, which the

Crown Princess must resign herself to. For example, she can no longer move about on her own. Shortly before the engagement, Mary was allocated her own bodyguard.

'She became very nervous because paparazzi photographers were following her. And if she crossed against an amber light, they crossed the red light in order not to lose her, and she was worried about that. For as she said, "They will either hit me or hit someone else." We had to handle that situation. We didn't ask for it. It was the police who had to evaluate if it was relevant and they thought it was,' says Per Thornit. Two bodyguards now follow the Crown Princess as soon as she leaves her private apartment and enters the public arena. When she is out on an official errand, a lady-in-waiting also always accompanies her.

And there are of course also a number of rules that a newly educated crown princess has to adhere to.

'Much comes from the home, but there are of course special rules of conduct for this house,' says Per Thornit. 'It is important to tell her how she is expected to behave in connection with official engagements. We have just had a state visit from Romania and from Luxembourg, which she attended, and of course in these cases she had to know where to walk and where to stand. And where do the members of the royal family stand and what happens and how do you walk there and there? And then you go to dinner there, and what do you do afterwards? We're talking about matters of procedure, arrangements that she, and everybody who's involved, must know.'

Life as a crown princess also means a place in the media spotlight with an inquisitive press nipping at her heels, watching over and commenting on her every move. Per Thornit and his student have talked a lot about that side of her life as a crown princess.

'She is quite relaxed in relation to the media and the press. She does not feel it's a strain on her or feel hard-pressed by it. She has a very rational attitude to it. We have of course talked about it because it will become a part of her everyday life – it is not something that is there now and then will disappear again. You can't just say, "It's over now," because it isn't. It is intense and it will be intense for the first couple of years, and then it may level out, but it will always be there. But she does not get angry or nervous or annoyed with them. She simply doesn't,' says Thornit.

Crown Princess Mary is very aware of her new role.

'The most important thing is that she is herself. If we manipulate that away from her and teach her to play a role, it will go wrong. We can't do that. Insincerity will show through right away. She must remain as she is and in addition there are some ground rules, but they are not all that different from those of many other places in society – so all will be well. She must not stray from being true to herself. We must be careful not to do that. We're not about to do that and we do not wish to either,' says Thornit.

There is no doubt that the transition from the normal life of a commoner to the life of a princess may be quite a task, even for a mature, intelligent and considered woman like Mary Donaldson.

'It can be difficult,' says Thornit, who acknowledges that his job also entails providing a shoulder for her to lean on. 'It is a tremendous transition, but I have tried it once before with Hong-Kong born Princess Alexandra. She came from almost as far away as one could come, and knew very little about Denmark. You come from a completely foreign country with a completely different response pattern, and even if we think we are alike, it is hardly the case. I think they have concealed it very well; it is a bit harder than we think.'

According to the Lord Chamberlain, there are several common features in the way Princess Alexandra and Crown Princess Mary have handled the transition from being female commoners to princesses. 'They both attacked it with determination, and they wanted to succeed. They made an effort.'

The fact that Mary has thought deeply about her future role and the possibility of having an influence on the monarchy became apparent in an interview with the journalist Ninka in *Politiken* only five days before her marriage to Frederik. 'The monarchy must show intelligence. There must be a warm, positive feeling surrounding it. Honesty. Foresight. Things should not just be done the way they have always been done because society is not as it has always been. One must be wise enough to realise the necessity for change. You have to follow the times. You can't just be a "ribbon cutter", you must also think strategically. You must be able to "read the market trends" and find the direction in which you want to go in order to become "relevant" in the "market".' Mary's remarks were also testament to her impatience to get started in her new role. She felt that she was in a kind of limbo while serving her apprenticeship.

'The development of society points to a more level structure, with the result that the royal family can no longer maintain the same role as before. That's why I believe that the royals must be wise enough to see how they can continue developing a strategy for survival,' said Mary.

Chapter 6

CONNECTIONS

Once upon a time there was a prince who wanted a princess, but it had to be a real princess. So he travelled the world to find such a princess, but everywhere he went there was something wrong. There were princesses enough, but whether they were real princesses he could not say. There was always something that was not right.

Thus starts Hans Christian Andersen's wonderful fairytale 'The Princess and the Pea', which has been read to millions of young children and which now has a whole new meaning. The Danish Crown Prince did travel to a foreign land to find his princess, and he found a Tasmanian princess with Scottish ancestry, a big heart, a happy smile and an academic education – the fairytale has become real. And when the two-hundredth anniversary of Hans Christian Andersen's birth was celebrated in Australia in April 2005, marvellous threads of connection were spun around exactly that fairytale.

The marriage between Crown Prince Frederik and Mary Donaldson is the icing on the cake in a longstanding relationship between Denmark and Australia. The Opera House, Sydney's world-famous landmark and architectural treasure, has a Danish lineage – it was designed by Danish architect Jørn Utzon. So it is fitting that Mary and Frederik's wedding was celebrated with a Danish–Australian party on the waterfront at the Opera House, symbolising that an exciting alliance has been forged which will in turn create new ties of culture, trade and friendship between the two nations.

Hans Christian Andersen's anniversary in 2005 was also celebrated in the Opera House. As patron for the Hans Christian Andersen jubilee year, Crown Prince Frederik has appointed the Australian world champion in the 400-metres sprint, the Olympic gold-medal winner Cathy Freeman, as ambassador for the Hans Christian Andersen anniversary year in Australia.

The threads of connection between the two fairytales were given yet another dimension when Frederik and Mary undertook their first official state visit to Australia in February and March 2005. The Crown Prince couple combined the state visit with the Hans Christian Andersen jubilee, and in addition to attending a gala performance at the Opera House, with Cathy Freeman present, Frederik and Mary travelled to Tasmania, where the Hans Christian Andersen anniversary year was also marked.

The vast majority of the approximately 10,000 first-generation Danes who live permanently in Australia are wild about the royal Danish–Australian connection. Many of these expatriate Danes are married to Australians. How is Mary's story being received in these circles?

'There is clearly a "Mary effect",' says Inger-Lise Goyne with a smile. She still speaks with a Danish accent from the island of Funen, even though she has spent half her life in Australia – first in Melbourne and then for more than twenty years in Tasmania, where she is now an active member of the Scandinavian Association and is busily engaged in arranging various Scandinavian festivals. 'The Danish traditions must be kept alive, and we are about 35 Danes in Hobart, who keep in contact via the Scandinavian club,' says Inger-Lise, whose three grown-up children have true Danish names: Per, Kirsten and Andreas. Her son Andreas, called Andrew, is best friends with Mary's brother, John.

'John has spent many evenings in this house, jamming with Andrew and other boys. They are old and close friends and have always kept in contact even though today John lives many thousands of kilometres away. He is a wonderful boy, but it is a very private family. They don't make a lot of fuss over their daughter marrying a royal, and we must respect that,' says Inger-Lise.

The girl from Funen enjoys life in Tasmania, and she does not mind admitting that she is interested in Mary and Frederik as royal celebrities. But she also says that people in Tasmania are unfazed by the fact that their own Mary will become the next Queen of Denmark.

'Tasmanians are completely unsnobbish and difficult to impress. They are honest and very relaxed. The tempo is different to the rest of Australia, and people are loyal to their families and this fantastic island,' says Inger-Lise. She has herself lost her heart to Tasmania and thinks that Funen pales a little in comparison.

The first Dane to set foot on Tasmanian soil was probably the young ship's officer Jørgen Jürgensen in 1803. The New South Wales governor, Philip King, had commissioned Lieutenant John Bowen to establish a settlement in Van Diemen's Land, as it was then known. Bowen's party left Port Jackson in the brig *Lady Nelson* and the whaler *Albion* in late August 1803. First officer on *Lady Nelson* was the 23-year-old Jørgen Jürgensen, son of a watchmaker to the court in the King's city, Copenhagen. Jørgen Jürgensen was kicked out of school, accused of being a troublemaker, and decided to seek adventure on the high seas. In addition to the crew, there were 24 convicts on board. On Friday 9 September 1803 first officer Jürgensen gave the order to drop anchor in Ralphs Bay at the mouth of the Derwent River. The hills were green and fertile and in the distance a snow-covered mountain rose to a height of 1200 metres. Later, the mountain was named Mount Wellington, and Jørgen Jürgensen was with the first European expedition that climbed to its summit.

Jürgensen sailed back to Sydney, and a few months later he returned to the settlement with a new load of convicts, who were going to help build the new colony. Later in the year, Jürgensen helped establish a whaling station at Ralphs Bay.

In Denmark, little is known of first officer Jørgen Jürgensen, but he has inscribed himself in a long and colourful chapter in the history of Tasmania. As fate would have it, Jørgen Jürgensen left Australia and went north, where this soldier of fortune proclaimed himself King of Iceland and ruled for 100 days. After that, the ex-King lived in Denmark and then England, where he made a living as a writer, theologian and doctor, and later as a swindler. Jørgen Jürgensen was caught in 1826 and transported to Van Diemen's Land. In his diary notes from the time he describes how it was to return to the colony that he himself had helped establish.

Jürgensen spent the rest of his life on the island where, as a leader of expeditions, he helped to explore unknown territory and crossed the wilderness from south to north. His detailed measurements and descriptions were to play a role in the establishment of European land routes across the island.

Jørgen Jürgensen also took part in the horrifying 'Black War', a series of conflicts between white settlers and Tasmanian Aboriginal people. The Danish adventurer died in Hobart in January 1841, and the memory of him is alive and well in Tasmania. He is the subject of several historical biographies and his face is one of those carved into the arches of the historic convict-built bridge at Ross in Tasmania's midlands.

Even though the history of Denmark has unfolded in a very different way to that of Australia, it is striking that Australians are much more enthusiastic about the Scandinavian countries than they are about the USA, for instance. That is also the impression that the Danish Consul General in Australia, Jørgen Møllegård, has; in his experience, Australians can't get enough of Denmark.

'Jørn Utzon is a hero here, and it is to his credit that all Australians know of Danish design and architecture. Utzon has opened the eyes of the Australians to the Danish design and lifestyle, and combined with the "Mary effect", we're experiencing a boom in interest in Danish products and Danish culture, music and films,' says Jørgen Møllegård.

Jewellery from Georg Jensen, furniture from Fritz Hansen, kitchen-ware from Bodum, TV sets and music centres from Bang & Olufsen, lamps from Louis Poulsen, clothes from Bruun's Bazar, Day and Naja Lauf: Australians have discovered Mary's new country. In addition to Jørn Utzon and Hans Christian Andersen, the most famous Dane 'Down Under' is without a doubt Crown Prince Frederik. A few years ago Australians did-n't know anything about the Danish royal family, but Frederik's romance with and marriage to an Australian woman has all of a sudden made him famous throughout the country.

The film director Lars von Trier is also known to Australians, perhaps because he gave Nicole Kidman the lead role in his film *Dogville*. And just as most Danes know the Australian actors Russell Crowe and Mel Gibson and pop star Kylie Minogue, many Australians also know Danish soccer legend Michael Laudrup and actor Viggo Mortensen.

'Danes are very popular here in Australia, and we have some traits in common ... it is a defining common feature between Australians and Danes that we like to create a friendly atmosphere,' says Jørgen Møllegaard.

It is easier for Australians to identify with Scandinavians than with other Europeans or Americans, says the Sydney manager of the

Scandinavian travel agency My Planet, Greg Arnott. Arnott, an Australian who has lived in Sweden and Denmark for some years, is wild about Denmark, and he is now marketing the Kingdom of Denmark as Mary's new country in order to attract Australians to Scandinavia. Greg Arnott is in no doubt that Australian tourists will completely fall for Denmark, and in his opinion Scandinavia is an undiscovered tourism gem, on account of its nature, culture and history, but also because he sees Scandinavians and Australians as very alike.

'Our biggest common feature is that we do not apply double standards. Americans and many Europeans take themselves too seriously and show double standards in relation to religion, marriage, sexuality, etc. Australians and Scandinavians are more straightforward and honest. We are ironic and informal. We laugh a lot, we do not judge people by the way they dress, and we can enjoy a beer with the neighbour, no matter what his title is,' says Arnott.

The former pastor at the Danish Church in Sydney, Torben Ebbesen, agrees. 'Australians like Danes, because we are straight talkers and we are not affected. That's how they are themselves. Australians have what they call the "tall poppy syndrome", which is a bit like the Danish "Law of Jante". They love it if an ordinary person can achieve something great, but at all costs you must avoid becoming a braggart, who can no longer have a beer with ordinary people. They are very proud of Aussies who have put their country on the world map. But don't think you are somebody just because you have made it. If you become a snob and lose contact with reality, you are likely to be cut down to size, and people will lose their respect for you. Australians are proud of their high achievers in sport, music and the dramatic arts. But if you think too much of yourself, there is no respect left,' says Ebbesen.

According to the Danish Law of Jante – just as in the tall poppy syndrome – you must not think you're something special, right from the start.

Mary and Frederik attending Prince Henrik's 70th birthday celebrations,
Copenhagen, June 2004

Queen Margrethe, Frederik, Mary and Prince Henrik watch the
women's handball at the Athens Olympics, August 2004

Mary attending a reception at London's Royal Academy of Arts, September 2004

Mary at the opening ceremony of Danish parliament, Copenhagen, October 2004

Torben Ebbesen believes that will also apply to Mary, if she is to avoid being cut down by the tall poppy syndrome.

When Queen Margrethe was on an official visit to Australia in 1987, she attended a Danish Church service in Sydney, and when Crown Prince Frederik and Prince Joachim attended the Olympics in 2000 they visited the church too. In addition to holding services and performing religious ceremonies for Danes throughout Australia, the church in the suburb of Pennant Hills also functions as a social and cultural rallying point for resident Danes and the many tourists who visit Australia every year.

'Australian society is very much like the Danish, and that is why the Danes find it so easy to integrate. We have almost no second-generation Danish migrants, because the Danes very quickly establish a network of Australian friends, and they do not live in ghettos where they only mix with each other,' says Torben Ebbesen.

Even if the Danes settle into Australian society quickly and easily, many frequent the Danish Church for services, christenings, confirmations and weddings. And in the Danish community hall behind the church, news and gossip from home is exchanged regularly. Young backpackers also use the church hall as a meeting place. For Christmas in 2003, the church's then assistant pastor, Anders Kaufmann Jensen, served Danish-style roast pork and home-baked brown cakes and almost 50 young people who were 16,000 kilometres from home danced around the Christmas tree so they could celebrate Danish Christmas traditions away from home.

According to Torben Ebbesen, the royal alliance is of great interest to Danes in Australia, whether they live in Perth, Brisbane or Sydney. It amuses Torben Ebbesen to compare the royal wedding to a typical Australian wedding.

'Whether we talk about weddings or other events like birthdays, the Australians celebrate these in a very different way to the Danes. According to Danish tradition, the dinner lasts many hours with obligatory speeches in a particular order and many party songs ... When the Danish royal family hosts an official dinner, it is of course very formal, stiff and protracted ... The party culture in Australia is relaxed and has less ceremony than in Denmark,' says Ebbesen.

Throughout history, most Danish Queens have come from abroad, and as propagators of culture and bridge-builders between nations, they have been agents of change. Most Danish Queens were born into noble houses and were brought up to carry on royal traditions. Queen Ingrid was descended from the Swedish royal family and knew what her royal role would entail. She became her contemporaries' connection across the Sound between Denmark and Sweden, and just six months before her death, the physical bridge was opened that now connects the two countries.

Crown Princess Mary will also become her contemporaries' bridge-builder, forging fresh connections between the island of her birth and her new home.

Chapter 7

HEART OR THRONE

It was the wedding of the century. Over one billion people followed the ceremony on TV and radio, and many hundreds of thousands followed the event in the streets of London when Lady Diana on 29 July 1981 was married to the heir to the British throne, Prince Charles, in St Paul's Cathedral. Diana was now Princess of Wales, and the wedding day was celebrated in workplaces over the whole of Great Britain and with street parties in even the smallest village. All the shops were decorated with portraits of the couple.

The wedding was followed closely in Commonwealth countries. In Australia a nine-year-old girl sat glued to the TV screen.

'I remember the wedding very well. The most impressive memory is the picture where she had this very long train and when she walked up the red carpet, but I can't remember that I was thinking of becoming a princess myself,' Mary Donaldson confessed to the Danish media.

Twenty-three years later, that Australian girl stood herself as a bride at a lavish royal wedding attended by crowned heads of state, in the world's oldest monarchy.

Mary's memories of Princess Diana probably also contain the sad ending of the fairytale about a woman who fell for a crown prince but who could not settle into the role of princess. It is one thing to have to make an indelible impression on one's future husband, his parents and family but to fall for a crown prince is something quite different – at least for a girl who is not born with blue blood in her veins. There is a whole nation that has to be convinced about the future bride's outstanding qualities. A whole country that demands to know everything about the future crown princess. And besides that, an unremitting press who will dig into all facets of her previous life.

Many others before Mary have with more or less success completed the process of becoming a crown princess, even if they grew up as ordinary girls. Perhaps they even had dreams of becoming a princess; a pink dress-up frock at home in the cubbyhouse.

The last centuries have seen radical changes in the European royal houses. On the whole, all princes and princesses today marry commoners. They are no longer bound by rules of aristocracy and traditions to find a partner within the other European royal houses. Today, it is the norm rather than the exception that princes and princesses fall in love with ordinary people and that they are permitted to marry their chosen ones without having to relinquish the right to the throne. That would have been unthinkable just 70 years ago. Then, it was a choice between heart or throne if a crown prince fell in love with a non-aristocrat, as was the case with the British King Edward VIII in 1936 who chose to abdicate to follow his heart and marry the divorced American Wallis Simpson.

Today a storm of popular protests would be heard if Queen Margrethe or a council of state were to deny Frederik permission to marry the love of his life on the grounds that she hails from an ordinary family. In a time when royals attend normal schools and colleges and are integrated into society from childhood, the royals must of course also have the freedom to marry for love.

All Frederik's contemporaries in other European royal houses and most of his cousins have married commoners. So Frederik did what other royals are doing – he followed his heart. Members of the nobility and princes from European states have for centuries married for strategic and political reasons but this tradition has been completely broken today. It also means that royals become less and less royal, as they marry and have children with commoners. And the freedom to follow one's heart also makes the monarchies more vulnerable, as is the case in Norway and Holland, where the Crown Princes have married young women of controversial backgrounds.

In comparison to the other European royal houses, the Danish royal family – or rather the Danish constitution – is rather out of date when it comes to equal right to the throne for boys and girls. In Norway, Sweden, Belgium and Holland, laws were passed which allow females to accede to the throne if they are the first born. And crown princesses who are also commoners in Norway, Belgium and Holland have within the last few years all borne girls, who in time will become reigning queens in their homelands. If Mary and Frederik's first child is a daughter, she becomes heir to the throne, but if she later on has a little brother, he takes over as heir to the throne, and his older sister must be content with playing second fiddle. This is at variance with the general perception of Denmark as a society that is the pioneering country of equality.

Mary doesn't have to look far for help and support from other commoner princesses, crown princesses and queens who have also experienced insecurity, doubt and perplexity in their difficult role. First and foremost, Mary can learn from Princess Alexandra. The Hong Kong-born Alexandra has an extraordinary natural talent for attending to her royal duties and being a patron, and she has taken very easily and professionally to her new role. The Danes love and respect Alexandra, and Mary will be able to draw on her experiences to settle in to her own role.

In both the Swedish and Norwegian royal families, the Crown Princes married commoners in the 1960s and 1970s who also became popular as queens in spite of initial resistance and scepticism from many old-fashioned royalists.

Twenty-eight years before the Sydney romance between Frederik and Mary started, the young Swedish Crown Prince, Carl Gustav, met the woman of his choice during the Olympic Games in Munich in 1972. The 29-year-old Silvia Sommerlath was a hostess at the Games, but after their first meeting almost four years had to pass before Silvia Sommerlath and Crown Prince Carl Gustaf could go public with their engagement.

During that time the Crown Prince became King. On 15 September 1973 the Swedish King Gustaf IV Adolf died and the 27-year-old Crown Prince acceded to the throne as King Carl XVI Gustaf. With his motto 'For Sweden – in my time' the King announced that he intended to strive to fulfil the demands which society would place on a modern monarch.

But Silvia Sommerlath was still in his thoughts and in 1976, the engagement was announced. The Swedish newspaper *Aftonbladet* described what happened:

'The King and Silvia have had many things to consider. Could Silvia as an "ordinary" woman take the pressure and adjust to the role of queen?

'The King asked his uncle, Prince Bertil, for advice. He had met Silvia several times, and he answered without hesitation, "If you don't marry her, you are an idiot. The Swedish people will love her."

'And then they sat there on a sofa in front of all the reporters, and one of them asked what Silvia had that no other girl had. "She is Silvia," the King answered. And Silvia was asked if she had any particular queen as a model, and she answered as quickly as lightning: "No, but I have a King."

'Prince Bertil was of course right. The Swedes surrendered.'

Three months later, Silvia Sommerlath became Queen Silvia of Sweden when she married King Carl XVI Gustaf of Sweden in the Stockholm Cathedral. Silvia's stylish demeanour has won her respect, and at the end of the 1990s the republican organisation in Sweden had only 170 members. The girl of the people had won both the King and the kingdom.

The Swedish royal couple has three children, Crown Princess Victoria, Prince Carl Philip and Princess Madeleine. According to the Swedish law of succession of 1980, the eldest child will inherit the throne. So in Sweden, they can expect a prince consort who is also a commoner when Crown Princess Victoria one day marries. Victoria, Carl Philip and Madeleine's sweethearts are all commoners.

Back in the 1960s, the then Crown Prince Harald of Norway fell for a girl of the people. But he had to wait even longer than his Swedish colleague for the woman of his choice.

Sonja Haraldsen from Oslo was a secondary school graduate with training as a dress and suit maker when as a 22-year-old she first met the Norwegian Crown Prince Harald at a private party. For several years rumours circulated about the Crown Prince and a girlfriend who was a commoner – mostly in the foreign press, because the Norwegian press was very reticent to write about the affair. When Norwegian papers finally wrote about the romance, the court denied everything. A commoner bride was out of the question. Several European princesses were introduced as possible crown princess candidates, but the rumours continued.

In the meantime, Sonja Haraldsen went to Switzerland, where she graduated at the finishing school l'Ecole Professionelle de Jeunes Filles in Lausanne.

According to a Norwegian biography about King Olav, the Crown

Prince eventually delivered an ultimatum: either he would be allowed to marry the woman he loved, or he would live as a bachelor for the rest of his life. In March 1968 – almost nine years after the couple's first meeting – the president of the Norwegian parliament, The Storting, Bernt Ingvaldsen, at last announced that King Olav had given his permission to an engagement between the Crown Prince and Miss Sonja Haraldsen. But it was after deep considerations, the King said later.

'The decision to give Harald permission to marry a commoner was of course not easy,' said the King, who had conferred with his government and members of parliament. 'One has to try to consider the young people who are involved,' he said in an interview at the end of the 1970s. The engagement caused a robust debate about the future of the Norwegian monarchy. But the opposition to the Crown Prince marrying a commoner was far less than many had feared, and it subsided when Sonja Haraldsen became Crown Princess Sonja. In August 1968 Sonja and Crown Prince Harald were married in Oslo Cathedral, and the Norwegians accepted and came to be very fond of their new Crown Princess. After King Olav's death in 1991, Harald became King and Sonja, Queen. The royal couple has two children, Princess Märtha Louise, who was born in 1971, and Crown Prince Haakon, who was born in 1973.

History repeated itself with renewed strength when Crown Prince Haakon in 1999 fell in love with Mette-Marit Tjessem Højby. Here, as mentioned earlier, it was the lifestyle of the bride that triggered the debate. Mette-Marit Tjessem Højby didn't have any impressive degrees or any practical work experience to take with her to her new life as a crown princess. She was a child of divorced parents, had moved with ease in scenes with easy access to illegal drugs, and she had been engaged to a man who was sentenced for possession of 50 grams of cocaine, other drug offences, violence and drink-driving. And on top of that, she was a single mother.

Mette-Marit Tjessem Højby met Crown Prince Haakon during a music festival in her home town, Kristiansand, in the summer of 1999. Shortly before Christmas the relationship became public knowledge, and in May 2000 the Crown Prince confirmed his love for Mette-Marit on TV. In September 2000, the court announced that Crown Prince Haakon had bought a flat in Oslo, and that he would move in with Mette-Marit Tjessem Højby and her three-year-old son, Marius. The Crown Prince was going to be a stepfather. Yet another taboo had been broken.

During the engagement period, Mette-Marit had a few official duties, but accepting a single mother with a somewhat shady past was a big ask for the Norwegian public. At a press conference a few days before the wedding, the future Crown Princess laid the cards on the table herself:

'Since it has become public knowledge that I am the Crown Prince's girlfriend, there have been a few rumours about my past ... I think my youthful rebellion probably was a bit more explosive than that of others. At the time it was important for me to live contrary to what was acceptable. That also led to my living a rather dissolute existence. I was part of a milieu where we had to try things and we crossed some boundaries. It was a hard-earned experience for me, which has taken me a long time to come to terms with. So that there is no doubt about where I stand today I take this opportunity to say that I distance myself from narcotics.'

In August 2001 the couple married in Oslo Cathedral with Europe's heads of state and royals among the guests. Denmark's Crown Prince Frederik was best man. He was there on his own. No one knew about his secret love on the other side of the world.

After the wedding, no one was in doubt. Reporting from the celebrations, *The Times* of London wrote that the wedding of the Crown Prince in Oslo had strengthened the monarchy in Norway. It had even become a test of strength that ended in a triumph for the newlyweds, the royal couple and the kingdom. Mette-Marit Tjessem Høiby won a convincing victory. She was breathtakingly beautiful, and the looks she and the Crown Prince exchanged throughout left no one in doubt that they were enchanted by each other. Another explanation for the day being a triumph was – according to *The Times'* reporter – that none of the key figures tried to avoid the issues. Both Oslo's bishop, who officiated at the wedding, and the father of the bridegroom, the King, acknowledged that it had possibly not been a textbook royal wedding.

The Norwegians had also taken their Crown Princess into their hearts. Some 120,000 people – every fourth inhabitant of Oslo – had positioned themselves along the bride and groom's route through the city.

The Norwegian newspaper *Dagbladet* had called for this to be the last royal wedding in Norway, and stated that the country had to become a republic very soon, but on the wedding day the newspaper was a lonely cry in the wilderness, wrote *The Times*.

The Crown Princess's four-year-old son, Marius, made an impression on all who followed the wedding. All through the day he was never far from the centre of events. And when the married couple watched the gigantic fireworks from the palace's balcony, it was Crown Prince Haakon who picked little Marius up in his arms so he could have a better view. The Crown Prince was deeply in love, and his speech to his bride brought tears to the eyes of even the most hardened:

> *I don't think I have ever been so weak or so strong as I am when I am with you.*
>
> *I don't think I have been so full of love as I am when I'm with you.*
>
> *From today you are no longer just my friend, my girlfriend and my fiancée. Today we have married and you have become Norway's Crown Princess.*

I'm looking forward to working side by side with you, and with Marius. I cannot promise it will be without problems and easy, but it will be eventful and strong.

Thank you for giving me the opportunity to live with Marius. That is a gift in itself.

Thank you for your love and for your contribution, Mette-Marit. I am proud of being able to call myself your partner for life.

Because we are here now. We are together now.

Mette-Marit, I love you!

I would like to propose a toast to the bride.

The Norwegians had to surrender and accept Crown Princess Mette-Marit, as the Crown Prince had done.

But Mette-Marit's past still haunts her even today. Her father has announced that he intends to write a book about his grandchild Marius, against the wishes of Mette-Marit. A music video with compromising shots of Mette-Marit from her wild past suddenly surfaced. And her older brother was convicted for violence against his ex-girlfriend. In each case, Mette-Marit's name was mentioned. In the autumn of 2002 the royal couple chose to settle in London – officially to study, but in reality to give Mette-Marit some peace to get used to her new shared role. In the summer of 2002 the Crown Princess said: 'Only one year has passed since I became Crown Princess, and I have used this time to become comfortable in my new role. I have to live with it for the rest of my life.'

The royal couple has also responded to the media's often relentless hunt for news about Mette-Marit, her family and her past. They returned to Norway in the autumn of 2003, and on 21 January 2004 they had their first child, Princess Ingrid Alexandra, who will become the first female regent of Norway for more than 600 years when she one day succeeds her father.

In the spring of 2004, Crown Prince Haakon took the opportunity at the birth of Princess Ingrid Alexandra to meet with the Norwegian press to discuss the boundaries for coverage of the royals' private lives. The Crown Prince wanted an agreement with the press to protect the children. 'That is something my parents did for my sister and me when we were little. We want to do the same,' Crown Prince Haakon said to the Norwegian trade journal *Journalisten*.

The Crown Prince was generally satisfied with the media coverage of the royal family. But he took the opportunity to point out where the boundaries for coverage of the royal family lay. He asked that the media refrain from photographing inside the royals' private premises, and he wanted the family to be able to move about alone without being shadowed by the press. Only time will tell whether this will happen.

The Norwegian royal house, and especially Mette-Marit, is under constant bombardment and pressure from the media and even from within. Books questioning the Norwegian monarchy's future and demands for transparency concerning the royal house's accounts are further symptoms of Norwegians' critical attitude to the way their royals behave.

Feelings ran high in Holland in 2001 when Crown Prince Willem-Alexander got engaged to the 29-year-old Máxima Zorreguieta from Argentina. Here, the educational and social background was in order, but in her case it was the family of the bride that gave rise to debate; more specifically Máxima's father, Jorge Horacio Zorreguieta, who was Minister for Agriculture during the Argentinian military dictatorship. The critics claimed that as a minister in the government from 1979 to 1981, he would not have been ignorant of the torture and executions that took place in Argentina. It is estimated that over the period 30,000 people died or disappeared.

Máxima grew up in Buenos Aires, where she was educated in economics at Universidad Católica Argentina in 1995. The couple met through mutual friends in Spain in 1999, at a time when Máxima Zorreguieta was working in New York. And after several visits, either to New York or Amsterdam, Máxima eventually told her parents about her boyfriend, whom she till then had described as a Dutch consultant by the name of Alexander. On Dutch TV, Máxima said how she had conveyed the news to her parents.

'He is a Dutch prince, not the youngest, but the eldest son of Queen Beatrix,' she told them. 'Are you crazy? You have your own life, you are independent. That's not for you,' was her parents' reaction. Two weeks later they arrived in New York to make sure their daughter was quite right in the head, but when they saw how happy Máxima was, they decided that Alexander must be the right one for her. Crown Prince Willem-Alexander proposed to Máxima on 19 January 2001. After a lovely afternoon where the Crown Prince had taught Máxima to skate, he enticed her to come to the side of the lake to a place where he had hidden roses and champagne. The Crown Prince had practised how to propose and he used English so he could be sure she would understand him. She did – and she said 'Yes' at once.

In March 2001, the engagement between the Prince of Orange, Crown Prince Willem-Alexander, and Máxima Zorreguieta was declared. The couple had then known each other for two years. In one of her very rare TV appearances, Queen Beatrix said that it was a great pleasure for her to announce the engagement. The Queen described Máxima as an intelligent, modern and courageous woman, who was faithful to all that was close to her. Máxima beamed after the Queen's announcement and said, 'I am happy that I can at last show myself in public with Alexander.'

A report supported by the government had concluded that Jorge Horacio Zorreguieta had not personally been involved in human rights violations. But the report also stated that it would have been unthinkable that Zorreguieta had been ignorant of the oppression.

According to the Crown Prince, the constant criticism of her father's relationship with Máxima had put pressure on the couple, '… but we have emerged stronger from it,' he said to the media, when the engagement became public. Máxima said that she regretted that her father had been a member of 'the wrong government', but that he had served with good intentions. About three months later, the Dutch government gave its consent to the marriage on the condition that Máxima's father did not attend the wedding. Máxima's father agreed after the Dutch Prime Minister, Wim Kok, had explained to him that it would be best for his daughter's future. Máxima called the decision painful, but understandable.

Máxima realised that her life would change dramatically. In a TV interview she said, 'You cannot say in advance what will happen to you, but I had a feeling about it.' Máxima was always aware of the public scrutiny. While she lived in New York, cameras were likely to be close to her home or her place of work. 'It is difficult to protect the people who are close to me. I had accepted that it was a consequence of my relationship with Alexander.' She added, 'You cannot stop untrue stories, but it is important to have a private life, because you need it.'

On 2 February 2002, they were married in Amsterdam in the presence of 1700 guests, among them Prince Charles, South Africa's President Nelson Mandela, the godmother of the bridegroom, the Danish Queen Margrethe – and Crown Prince Frederik. Yet again he was without his sweetheart by his side, even though Mary at that time had left Australia to be closer to Frederik.

But in the middle of all Máxima's happiness there was no doubt that she was grieving over not being able to share the biggest day of her life with her close family. And her feelings gave way when Carel Kraayenhof played the Argentinian tango 'Adiós Nonino' ('Goodbye father') on the special tango harmonica during the wedding ceremony.

The people of Amsterdam and the city itself were dressed in orange to greet the newlyweds after the ceremony, but there were a few who did not appreciate the new Dutch–Argentinian connection. Eggs were thrown at the bridal couple when they drove through the city after the wedding.

The couple had their first child on 7 December 2003. Princess Catharina-Amalia Beatrix Carmen Victoria, called Princess Amalia, will become Holland's future Queen, when she one day succeeds her father.

Belgium is the European kingdom where events quietly took their course when the Crown Prince got engaged to a commoner. The heir to the throne, Prince Philippe, was 39 years old when in 1999 he married the 26-year-old speech therapist Mathilde d'Udekem d'Acoz. Mathilde is descended from an aristocratic family. Her parents are the Count and Countess d'Udekem d'Acoz. She is the eldest of five siblings and grew up in a castle, Losange in Bastogne in the Flemish-speaking part of Belgium. After her graduation from secondary school, she started studying to become a speech therapist at the Marie-Haps Institute. Mathilde's grandmother, Princess Sofia Sapieha-Kodenska died in 1997 in a traffic accident together with Mathilde's older sister, Marie-Alix. At that time, Mathilde had already met Prince Philippe, but the relationship developed after the accident.

When Prince Philippe succeeds to the throne after King Albert, Mathilde will become the first Belgian-born Queen in the country. Mathilde has managed the upheaval from speech therapist to Crown Princess without much trouble. She hasn't put a foot wrong and she is praised for her stylish and graceful demeanour. The couple has two children. Princess Elisabeth was born in October 2001, and in August 2003 the couple became parents to Prince Gabriel. In due course, Princess Elisabeth will become the first female head of state, after an amendment to the legislation that will guarantee female succession to the throne.

In Spain, the royal declaration of love came unexpectedly one quiet Saturday evening in November. The court announced that the country's 35-year-old Crown Prince, Felipe de Borbon, had become engaged five days earlier to the 31-year-old divorcee and TV journalist Letizia Ortiz Rocasolano.

No one had any inkling, not even the meddlesome Spanish media, which usually had a handle on the Crown Prince's female acquaintances. The night before the announcement, Letizia Ortiz hosted the national news bulletin on Spain's TVE.

Letizia and Crown Prince Felipe met when she was covering the catastrophic oil spill in connection with the sunken oil tanker *Prestige* off Spain's northern coast, and the Crown Prince came to inspect the damage and give moral support to the many volunteers who were engaged in the rescue work. They met again at a gala dinner in April 2003, where the war in Iraq was the big topic of conversation. Here, Letizia Ortiz had first-hand knowledge, because her TV station had posted her to Baghdad.

One week before the relationship became public knowledge, the Crown Prince visited TVE, but the couple did not reveal anything when Felipe was presented to the beautiful studio hostess.

They became officially engaged on 6 November. In front of their respective parents, 350 journalists and rolling TV cameras, Crown Prince Felipe gave the woman of his choice a ring of white gold and diamonds, while she gave him gold cufflinks with sapphires.

At the time, Letizia Ortiz said of the engagement that she had no plans to leave her job completely, but that she would gradually scale down and prepare herself for the wedding and the duties of a princess. 'It is clear that from now on I will gradually participate in and devote myself to my

DANSK
ERY DANISH

TION #06
RING SUMMER 2005

120.00
12.00
RO 16.00
22.00

Mary on the cover of *Dansk*, February 2005

Mary attending Copenhagen International Fashion Fair, February 2005

Mary and Frederik before racing yachts against each other on Sydney Harbour;
Mary won 2–1

Mary attending Victor Chang Royal Ball with sister Jane, Sydney, March 2005

new life and the obvious duties it includes, with the support of the King and the Queen,' she said.

War and catastrophe correspondent, admired studio hostess – and on top of that, a divorcee. But Letizia Ortiz had only been married for one year to her former literature teacher, so the Spaniards quickly forgave her, and the relationship had the King and the Queen's warm support.

Among Crown Prince Felipe's former relationships was the Norwegian model Eva Sannum and although they were a couple for almost three years, the non-Catholic model never obtained royal approval.

Only one week after Mary and Frederik's May wedding in Copenhagen, Crown Prince Felipe and Crown Princess Letizia said yes to each other in the Almudena church in Madrid.

The Japanese royals are at first glance part of a culture far removed from Denmark or Australia. But the problems that suddenly surfaced for the Japanese Crown Princess, Masako, might well have emerged in any of the European royal houses. Owada Masako was a career diplomat in the Japanese foreign ministry, educated at Harvard University in the US and at Oxford. She met Crown Prince Naruhito in connection with a visit by the Spanish royal family in 1986, when she accompanied the foreign visitors to a concert in the imperial palace. The story goes that the Crown Prince had even at that early meeting become enamoured of the young Masako, but that she was struck off the list of possible prospects because her grandfather was connected to a chemical concern that was involved in a large pollution scandal.

Masako was not easy to impress, but the Crown Prince was persistent, and in the end he was able to convince both Masako and the royal powers that be that she was the right one. When the engagement was declared in 1993, Masako said at the press conference that she was worried about life in the palace. 'But the Crown Prince, who knows of my worries, promised me that he will protect me with all his might,' the newly engaged Masako said.

The wedding was on 9 June 1993. The Japanese monarchy requires male succession to the throne, and Crown Princess Masako knew that the indisputable demand on her and the Crown Prince was to deliver a male heir. No boys have been born into the Japanese imperial family since Crown Prince Naruhito's little brother, Prince Akishino, was born in 1967. The imperial couple's third child is Princess Sayako (also called Princess Nori). And little brother Akishino's two children are girls.

The Japanese people eagerly anticipated news of the pitter-patter of little feet at the palace. After eight years and a traumatic miscarriage, Crown Princess Masako gave birth to a daughter on 1 December 2001. She was given the name Princess Aiko. It was a time of great happiness, but there was also the expectation that the next time it would be a boy ...

The pressures of her new life, so completely different to what she was used to, resulted in the Crown Princess becoming seriously ill in December 2003. In January 2004 she issued a statement in which she candidly admitted that her health had deteriorated because of the pressure of imperial life. 'Since I was married ten years ago, I have tried my best, under great pressure and in new, unfamiliar surroundings. But I have a feeling that my latest health problems are a result of accumulated physical and mental tiredness from that period,' the statement said.

Crown Princess Masako was spared all official duties for several months and the Japanese resumed discussion about female succession to the throne – because it looks as if no male child will be born into the family. To the magazine *Hello*, a high-ranking member of the imperial palace said that the subject is too politically sensitive. 'We cannot say officially that we are looking at the possibility, but we are and we would be negligent if we didn't do so.'

If Crown Prince Naruhito and Crown Princess Masako do not have a son in the foreseeable future, it may lead to one of the world's most conservative societies having to accept change and adopt a constitutional amendment that gives women the right to succeed to the throne. Opinion polls have long shown support for a revision, and there are supporters of an amendment among both the government and opposition MPs. It is almost 200 years since Japan last had a reigning empress. Altogether, eight empresses have ruled Japan in the 1500-year history of the Chrysanthemum Throne.

For Princess Diana, it wasn't her health but the marriage itself that succumbed to years of pressure in a stiff and unfeeling British royal house. Diana was married to one of the world's most sought-after bachelors, the heir to the British throne, but the relationship ended in divorce. Lady Diana Frances Spencer was the daughter of an earl, she grew up close to Queen Elizabeth's summer residence and as a child she played with the princes. But that background was no guarantee of success. The marriage didn't survive, in spite of Diana having been born almost a princess.

Diana's parents were divorced when she was eight years old. With her siblings, Diana lived with her father at Park House in Sandringham. When her grandfather, the Seventh Earl of Spencer, died in 1975, the family moved to the family property Althorp, in the English Midlands. The Spencer family and the royal family have known each other for many years. They were neighbours in Sandringham up to 1975, and on a fateful weekend in 1977, Prince Charles paid a visit to Althorp.

On 24 February 1981, the engagement between Lady Diana Spencer and Prince Charles was announced. The wedding was greatly anticipated. Prince Charles was by then 32 years old, and the media had linked him to several women before Lady Diana appeared on the scene. She was the first

British-born woman for more than 300 years to marry an heir to the British throne. It had hitherto been foreign women of royal descent who had attained that position.

Diana lived in a flat in Coleherne Court in London, and when her relationship with the British heir to the throne became known, the photographers' lenses followed her daily. She worked at a kindergarten, Young England School, in the suburb of Pimlico. Pictures of the shy Diana wearing an almost see-through skirt are still firmly fixed in the memories of many.

Just a year after the wedding, Princess Diana and Prince Charles had their first child. Prince William was born in 1982, and Prince Harry was born in 1984. But the marriage was never happy. Prince Charles had not forgotten the love of his youth, Camilla Parker Bowles – even though she had married someone else – and in December 1992 the court announced that the Prince and Princess of Wales had decided to separate. Royal scandal was a reality, and Queen Elizabeth described 1992 as an 'annus horribilis' for the monarchy.

In November 1995, Princess Diana talked in a TV interview about her problems, about Prince Charles's unfaithfulness and about the pressure of her public duties.

The Prince and Princess of Wales were formally divorced on 28 August 1996, but they shared duties and tasks in connection with the upbringing of their two sons, and as mother to the future heir to the throne, Prince William, Princess Diana continued to be regarded as a member of the royal family.

Princess Diana was well on her way to break free of the royal straitjacket and create a new life with a new man by her side, when on the night of 31 August 1997 she was killed in a traffic accident in Paris after a hair-raising car chase with the meddlesome news media who would never leave the princess alone. It was a tragic ending to the life of a princess. It seems that the combination of a young, vulnerable woman, an aggressive press, an expectant public and an unfaithful husband destroyed a woman's life.

One former commoner-turned-royal has already given some good advice to Mary on the new life that lies ahead for her. That is Princess Diana's once sister-in-law, Sarah, the Duchess of York. On 21 October 2003, shortly after the engagement between Mary Donaldson and Crown Prince Frederik, Sarah was a guest on CNN's chat show *Larry King Live*.

A viewer from Chicago called in:

Caller: Real quick question. I was wondering if you had any words of advice for Mary Donaldson, who is recently engaged to the crown prince of Denmark? Like you, she's lived on her own and had a career and [is] an independent woman. Do you have any advice when she assumes her royal role?'

Sarah Ferguson: The important advice I would ever give anyone is to say remain yourself. You have to be true to what you believe. Because then when the problems come or the obstacles come, you've got a very strong foundation. Like any good house, if you can keep a strong foundation, then the winds won't blow it down.

Larry King: What will be the roughest thing she'll face?

Sarah Ferguson: I don't know the kind of person she is, but I hope when the people might say some jibes or the press might turn ... always when you're leading up to a wedding, it's the honeymoon period, you believe everybody loves you ... then it turns after a couple of months. That's when it's difficult.

Mary is far from being the first crown princess in a European royal house who was once a commoner. And she certainly won't be the last.

Chapter 8

MARY'S MANY CASTLES

'Penthouse unit with three bedrooms, three bathrooms, two private parking spots, harbour promenade and a breathtaking view of Sydney Harbour Bridge.' 'Newly built, ultra-modern six-room timber cabin with all conveniences nestled in lush rainforest with direct views to the pristine blue waters near Port Douglas.' Or what about a country house surrounded by first-class vineyards, guesthouses, restaurants and a golf course in the Hunter Valley? All at prices on a scale that will only attract people who don't have to worry about money.

Through her last job in Sydney, Mary Donaldson became well acquainted with luxurious residences of the kind that most of us only dream about, let alone set foot in. The real estate company Belle Property, where Mary worked before she left Australia to move to Europe, specialises in first-class properties.

But Mary's knowledge of the luxury property market was mostly on a professional level. Her childhood home in Morris Avenue, Taroona, was an ordinary brick house of a size that without being ostentatious was very well suited to a family of six with the children sharing bedrooms.

Mary's own residences have been charming and cosy, but of a more modest standard. In Sydney, she shared accommodation with friends, first in the suburb of Paddington, later in the two-storey terrace in Porter Street in Bondi Junction, where she and Frederik first got to know each other out of the public's gaze.

As Crown Princess, Mary will have several imposing places in Denmark to choose from when she and the Crown Prince are going to establish themselves as a married couple.

First and foremost, the Chancellery house at Fredensborg castle close to Copenhagen in North Zealand – with its secluded position close to Esrom Lake, no doubt will become the couple's preferred private residence.

The Chancellery house is one of the extensions to Fredensborg castle. After the death of King Frederik in 1972, Queen Ingrid moved in and resided there for most of the year, until her death in November 2000. Now the house will become the base for Crown Prince Frederik and Crown Princess Mary's married life.

The Chancellery house, which was originally used as storage, was built in 1731, a little later than the castle itself, and prior to the wedding, it underwent a thorough renovation for 43 million kroner (AUD $9.2 million) to bring it up to date. Now the house appears simple and beautiful with freshly whitewashed walls and a new black glazed half hip-tiled roof. The Crown Prince moved into the Chancellery house in the spring of 2004, which gave him a month and a half head start to settle in and get organised before, as tradition decreed, he carried his bride over the threshold into their shared home.

Formally, Mary stayed in her flat at Langelinie in Copenhagen until the wedding, but of course she had a say in the furnishing of the couple's home.

The Chancellery house has plenty of room for a newlywed couple who must live in surroundings of a suitable standard in order to receive family and friends who arrive from foreign lands. The ground floor is 700 square metres and it encompasses, among other things, two beautiful domed halls. On the first floor is a further 450 square metres, and primarily consists of guestrooms and guest bathrooms. The division of the rooms has been retained as it was at the time of Queen Ingrid, but the bathrooms have been renovated, and a new kitchen has been built. Mary helped choose and fit it out.

In the grounds behind the Chancellery house, a new swimming pool has been constructed and the garden has been planted with a wealth of rhododendron bushes. Rhododendrons were among Queen Ingrid's favourite flowers and it is out of respect for his grandmother that the Crown Prince has chosen this beautiful spring flowering plant for his garden.

Normally, the royal house would be responsible for the costs in connection with internal maintenance, while the state through the Castle and Property Agency would be responsible for the exterior. But in the case of larger renovations, the state steps in. The Castle and Property Agency will take care of the fixtures of the building. For the Chancellery house, that means the kitchen and bathrooms, which were in need of renovation.

Construction manager for the Castle and Property Agency, Flemming Frydendahl, told *Berlingske Tidende* about the renovations. 'It was basically a nice house that Queen Ingrid left behind, but younger people have different needs and sense of colours. So we're talking about an internal renovation with painting, wallpapering and fitting out of, among other things, a big modern kitchen and several bathrooms.'

The Chancellery house has at the same time been effectively shielded from curious onlookers, and it has been fitted out with a state-of-the-art security system, which will guarantee the peace and privacy of the Crown

Prince and Princess. The security system, with its sophisticated alarms and surveillance cameras, is not only there to protect their private lives, but also to protect them against the security risk that a royal family is exposed to in a time of growing terror threats.

Beyond the Chancellery house and Fredensborg, which will be the ideal frame around the family life of the Crown Prince and Princess, Fredensborg castle is first and foremost the Queen and Prince Henrik's summer residence. When the days become longer, the magpies are singing and the light allows people to spend the evenings outdoors, the royal couple adjourn to the residence at Fredensborg, as it is known officially. The inhabitants of Fredensborg greet the couple with burning torches, and tradition calls for the Queen and Prince Henrik to step out onto the steps of the castle – wrapped in thick coats if it's one of the cold spring evenings – to say thank you for the welcome greeting. From early spring to late autumn, Fredensborg is the royal couple's home, only interrupted by the summer stay at the Marselisborg castle in northern Jutland, Gråsten castle in southern Jutland and the French vineyard castle near Cahors in the south of France.

Fredensborg castle is a pearl of baroque architecture. It was built as a hunting castle for Frederik IV in 1720, designed by the architect Johan Cornelius Krieger, and the name Fredensborg is due to the Big Nordic War which finished on 3 July 1720, while the castle was being built. In memory of the peace treaty, the castle was called Fredensborg, Castle of the Peace. Krieger was court gardener at Rosenborg castle and was chosen as the architect because Fredensborg was to be a castle where garden and castle functioned as a whole. And that is the case even today. The castle garden is open to the public all year round.

Under the reign of King Christian IX (1863–1906) and Queen Louise, Fredensborg really became the centre of royal family life. Every summer the royal couple gathered their children and children of their in-laws at Fredensborg castle. They were called 'Europe's in-laws', because through their six children, the family branched out to several of Europe's kingdoms and principalities. The eldest son, Prince Frederik, succeeded his father and later became King Frederik VIII; the eldest daughter, Princess Alexandra, married the British Prince Edward, later Edward VII; Prince Vilhelm became King of Greece, Princess Dagmar married the Russian Tsar Alexander III, Princess Thyra married the Duke of Cumberland, and the family of the youngest son, Prince Valdemar, branched out to the Romanian royal house.

It is at Fredensborg castle that many of the big events in the life of the royal family take place. Queen Margrethe and Prince Henrik's wedding party on 10 June 1967 was celebrated at Fredensborg castle with the bridal waltz in the domed hall, and the royal couple's silver wedding anniversary in 1992 was celebrated under marquees in the garden of Fredensborg. It was at Fredensborg that Prince Joachim and Princess Alexandra in a furious snowstorm celebrated their wedding on 18 November 1995. And of course it was here that Crown Princess Mary and Crown Prince Frederik celebrated their wedding on 14 May 2004.

It is also at Fredensborg castle that new ambassadors present their credentials to the Queen in the summer months, and where foreign heads of state are received during official visits in the summer. The guests stay at the castle and the official gala dinner for foreign guests is held in and transmitted on TV from the castle's domed hall with its beautiful star-patterned floor.

Tradition calls for the guests to sign Fredensborg's somewhat unusual guest book. Using a diamond, the visiting heads of state write their names on one of the castle's glass panes. And the old windowpanes attest to visits from, among others, the Russian heir to the throne Nikolai (Nicholas II of

131

Russia), Sir Winston Churchill and the former President of Germany Johannes Rau.

By taking up residence at the Chancellery house, Crown Prince Frederik relinquishes his big 600 square metre bachelor flat in Christian VIII's palace at Amalienborg.

But when Frederik or Mary have official duties in the capital or for other reasons want to stay in town, they still have a roof over their heads. The Queen has placed a flat in Christian VII's palace at Amalienborg at their disposal. They can use it until their own palace, Frederik VIII's palace, is ready to move into.

The couple's Lord Chamberlain, Per Thornit, explains: 'We are in the process of renovating Frederik VIII's palace, and it will take some time, because some of the most basic things like wiring and heating have to be replaced. Some of the installations go right back to the 1890s. It doesn't need painting but in a couple of years we would have to look at the old wiring and water pipes. So we'll do the whole lot now, otherwise the electricity and water will all of a sudden go, and that's no good. It will take a couple of years at least.'

Three to four years is the estimated time frame for the renovation of the 4700 square metre palace and the work is expected to cost 100 million kroner (AUD $21.5 million).

So even though Crown Prince Frederik and Mary have to wait a little while, they will in time be part of the tradition of crown princes and regents throughout Danish history, alternating between the four palaces at Amalienborg that surround the octagonal palace square and the equestrian statue of Frederik V, founder of Frederiksstaden, the part of the city where Amalienborg is situated.

Frederik VIII's palace is bigger than the residence that was made available for Princess Margrethe and Prince Henrik after their wedding in

1967. So the royal household of the Crown Prince and Princess will be extended, as there will be additional expenses in connection with the household – which was part of the rationale for increasing the appanage from the state to the Crown Prince.

Frederik VIII's palace, also called Brockdorff's palace, was built in the 1750s to 1760s. In 1869 the then Crown Prince Frederik moved into the palace, where he lived when in 1906 he became King Frederik VIII, thus giving the palace its current name. The latest renovation was in 1934, ahead of the wedding between the then heir to the throne Crown Prince Frederik and Crown Princess Ingrid. It, too, was a residence of Queen Ingrid until her death in November 2000 so, as at Amalienborg, Crown Prince Frederik is following in his grandmother's footsteps. And on another front Crown Prince Frederik will follow his grandmother. After Queen Ingrid's death, Queen Margrethe took over Gråsten castle, but she has announced that in time the Crown Prince will take over the castle.

The original Gråsten castle was built as a hunting castle in the 1500s. It burnt down several times, but the present castle has stood in the grounds since 1759. It has been renovated several times. After Germany invaded South Jutland in 1864, the castle, along with the rest of South Jutland, was occupied by the Germans. When most of South Jutland was reunified with Denmark in 1920, the state took over the castle and among other things it was used as a courtroom and residence for the local judge and chief constable of police.

After an extensive restoration, Gråsten castle was in 1935 handed over to the newlywed Crown Prince couple, Frederik and Ingrid, as a summer residence. They spent the summers at Gråsten, where Queen Ingrid established an imposing garden, with a lavish profusion of flowers inspired by romantic English landscape gardens. Gråsten is a living example of contemporary royal gardening art.

When King Frederik and Queen Ingrid's three daughters had grown up and started their own families, it was Gråsten that became the family's meeting place. With the family spread throughout Denmark, Germany and Great Britain, summers at Gråsten provided an opportunity for daughters, sons-in-law and ten grandchildren to meet and keep in contact with each other. Crown Prince Frederik has spent most of his summers at Gråsten with his cousins.

After Queen Ingrid's death, Queen Margrethe has kept the tradition alive by inviting her sons, sisters and their families for summer holidays at Gråsten every year. Mary has also visited Gråsten castle. *Billed-Bladet* reported that only a few hours after the Queen and Prince Henrik had arrived at the castle in July 2003, Mary and Frederik were the first of the family to move in. A large cavalcade of knights welcomed the Queen and Prince Henrik, but after the guests had departed the Crown Prince and his girlfriend arrived discreetly. When pictures were published of Mary on horseback in the Castle Park at Gråsten, accompanied by one of the royal family's staff members, it became clear that an engagement announcement was imminent.

The inhabitants of Gråsten hope to see much more of the Crown Prince and Princess. Gråsten Sailing Club has offered the Crown Prince, a keen sailor, a free spot in the harbour and an honorary membership of the sailing club. Crown Prince Frederik has accepted the offer, but the sailing club does not know if he wants to leave his Dragon class yacht in Gråsten harbour.

Gråsten castle is a favoured haven for the royal family, and when the royals are not staying at the castle, the gardens are open to the public. The castle chapel is open to the public all year round.

On the other hand, the royals can be by themselves completely when they visit the hunting lodge at Trend, and that has especially become a place where the Crown Prince has sought refuge when in need of peace and quiet. Trend lies in the western part of Himmerland, Jutland, near the eastern part of Limfjorden, with Farsø the closest town.

The royal family's hunting lodge was a present from the Danish people in 1935 to the then Crown Prince Frederik and Crown Princess Ingrid. King Frederik was fond of hunting, and he was host to many hunts for red deer at Trend. Today it is Crown Prince Frederik who invites his friends hunting at Trend. The hunting lodge is owned by a fund that is chaired by the Queen.

The Lord Chamberlain, Per Thornit, says that the Crown Prince is very fond of being at Trend.

'It is a lovely haven for him. He likes moving about in nature, and he can do that all alone, as it pleases him. He goes up there, not as often as he wants to, but regularly.'

Mary has accompanied Frederik to Trend several times. The couple spent New Year's Eve of 2002 in Trend with some good friends.

One of the other places where the Crown Prince couple will spend some time is on board the royal yacht, *Dannebrog*. Both Frederik and Mary love sailing. Mary has sailed with her friends in Australia, and Frederik is a respected yachtsman, who has reaped fine placings in Dragon racing championships.

It wasn't surprising then that it was from the sea that Mary saw her new homeland when she first moved about as Crown Princess.

The couple's first official tour went to the northernmost part of the kingdom, to Greenland, where together with Queen Margrethe and Prince Henrik they took part in celebrations for the twenty-fifth anniversary of self-government in Greenland.

Frederik even promised before he got engaged that he would show Greenland to his Queen. 'I'm certain I'll show my future wife around in

Greenland,' the Crown Prince said to the Greenland TV station, KNR, when he visited in May 2003.

Part of the visit was a cruise on board *Dannebrog*. The plan was for the royal family to sail to the capital, Nuuk (Godthåb), and up the west coast to Maniitsoq (Sukkertoppen), then on to Sisimiut (Holsteinsborg), Aasiaat (Egedesminde) and Qeqertarsuaq (Godhavn). From here they went on to Uummannaq and Qaarsut.

The royal yacht *Dannebrog* has sailed over 300,000 nautical miles since Queen Alexandrine, the wife of King Christian X (1912–47), christened it in 1931. The yacht has visited most of the harbours in Denmark, Greenland and the Faeroe Islands, but also other European countries, especially in France.

Dannebrog is both an official and a private residence of the Queen and Prince Henrik and members of the royal family when they are on official visits or on summer cruises in domestic waters. It was built at the naval dockyard in Copenhagen. The royal couple has studies, dining rooms, common rooms and bedrooms on board. When *Dannebrog* calls at Danish or foreign ports, the covered rear deck is used for receptions. The Queen's hunting captain commands *Dannebrog* and her crew of nine officers, seven sergeants and 36 national servicemen who have been especially selected from the navy.

After the visit to Greenland, Mary and Frederik again sailed on board *Dannebrog* in July 2004 when the Danes were given the opportunity to welcome their new Crown Princess. The summer cruise brought the Crown Prince couple to the towns of Aarhus, Odense and Sønderborg.

Mary attending the 90th anniversary gala dinner for the
Australian Red Cross, Sydney, March 2005

Huge crowds welcomed Mary everywhere on her 2005 Australian tour

Mary and Frederik greeting the crowds outside Sydney Opera House, March 2005

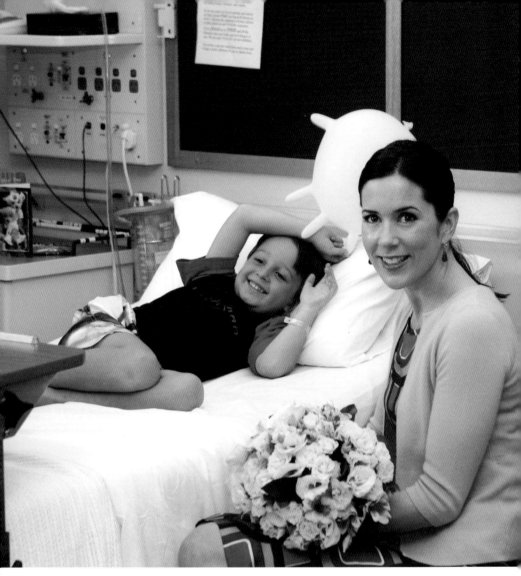

Mary visiting patients at Sydney's Westmead Hospital, March 2005

Chapter 9

YES

'Yes.' The hundreds of guests in Copenhagen's Cathedral, Vor Frue Kirke, could hardly hear the word. But Frederik heard it. And the TV microphones caught the word, so that millions of viewers the world over heard it. The moment belonged to Mary and Frederik. And there was no doubt that Mary's yes to Frederik was said with much love. Mary said yes to love and marriage. Yes to her destiny. Yes to the title of Crown Princess and everything that goes with it: the official duties, the representation, the glamour and the media attention. And yes to a new life and a future she had never aspired to, but which is part of the deal, when you lose your heart to a Danish crown prince.

Friday 14 May 2004 dawned a typical spring day – and a historic day for Denmark. The beech trees were so light green that they were almost blinding. The lilacs were ready to burst into bloom and send their intoxicating aroma over the country. It was a day the Danes will never forget. Copenhagen had been scrubbed for days, and all over the country women of all ages had indulged in their dreams of becoming a princess. They had bought tiaras in toy shops and arranged girls-only dinners in front of the

TV while they sent their men out to the kitchen. The suburban streets were empty when Mary stood as a bride in Denmark's royal wedding of the century, and it felt like the whole world was invited. People were there, either in front of the TV or in the front row in inner Copenhagen, where the paved streets and alleys were crammed with well-wishers who had taken up their positions already from early morning.

At half past two, Mary's tutor, Per Thornit, was already waiting in Copenhagen Cathedral for the Crown Prince and his future wife. Everything had to go like clockwork that day. It was the culmination of his coaching of Denmark's future Crown Princess. Mary's brother, John, and her sister-in-law, Leanne, also arrived early at Vor Frue Kirke together with Tasmanian brothers-in-law, Craig Stephens and Scott Bailey and nephews, Michael and Alexander. Mary's sisters and nieces had yet to arrive. They were to be bridesmaids and flower girls. When the members of the extended Scottish Donaldson clan arrived at the church, the strains of the Scottish hymn 'Fill thou my life, O Lord my God' were heard. Mary chose the hymn. The male members of the clan were all dressed in the traditional Scottish kilt. Mary's aunt Catherine Murray and her daughter Elizabeth and son-in-law Derek Syme represented Mary's late mother's branch of the family.

At half past three precisely, Crown Prince Frederik and his best man, Prince Joachim, arrived at the cathedral in Nørregade in the old part of central Copenhagen. When they alighted from the black Daimler limousine, Crown 1, the cheering crowd could be heard inside the church, where most of the wedding guests had already taken their places. The bridegroom was dressed in the gala uniform of the navy, wearing the Grand Order of the Elephant and the Star of the Order and the Cross of the Grand Commander. The gala uniform was new and had been sewn from 3.2 metres of Dowskind wool, and the Crown Prince was wearing King

Frederik IX's sword, given to him by Queen Ingrid in memory of his grandfather.

To the sounds of Carl Nielsen's 'The Festival Prelude' and Niels W. Gade's 'Morning Song' from *Elverskud*, 'The Sun Rises in the East' – two works by renowned Danish composers – a broadly smiling Crown Prince and his brother started the long walk up the aisle to the altar. The smile did not leave the lips of the Crown Prince. Seldom had he looked so happy, so much anticipating the sight of his Mary as a bride. The clear voices of the boys of the Copenhagen Boys' Choir made the eyes of the Crown Prince a little misty. Or perhaps he was thinking of Mary. For the Crown Prince, the next few minutes must have been like hours. Smiling, he whispered to Joachim. Looking … Shuffling … Waiting …

Then the royal guests arrived. They had almost all arrived by now: King Carl Gustaf and Queen Silvia of Sweden; King Harald and Queen Sonja of Norway; the Queen's sisters – Queen Anne-Marie and her husband, King Konstantin, Princess Benedikte and her husband, Prince Richard; the Netherlands' Queen Beatrix; and the Spanish Queen Sofia; all with their children and in-laws' children. The Belgian royal couple and the Grand Duke and Duchess of Luxembourg attended, as did Japan's Crown Prince, Naruhito, and Prince Edward and his wife, Sophie, the Countess of Wessex, from Great Britain. From Monaco came Prince Albert and his sister, Princess Caroline, with her husband, the German Prince Ernst August. The presidents of Iceland and Finland were there, along with the French president's wife, Bernadette Chirac, and Iran's ex-empress, Farah Pahlavi. Australia was officially represented by Governor-General Michael Jeffery, who was Queen Elizabeth's Australian representative, and Richard Butler, the then Governor of Tasmania.

Among the young royals who were present, some would no doubt have thought back to that evening in Sydney when the fairytale began; the

Crown Prince's Greek cousin, Nikolaos, and the Norwegian Princess Märtha Louise, along with Prince Joachim, were at the Slip Inn when Frederik met Mary.

The atmosphere in the cathedral was solemn. There were discreet exchanges of kisses on cheeks, and small nods. And the aroma of the colourful floral decorations was just as delicate and discreet. Together with the flower decorator Erik Buch, Queen Margrethe had given her directions for the floral arrangements, which had been designed in deference to the classical, pristine lines of the cathedral. Red roses with the varietal names of Black Magic and Red Unique were dominant, together with carnations in red, pink and orange tones. There were pink peonies and sweet peas, and there were bleeding hearts and buttercups. There were also Australian eucalyptus flowers, and by the altar and the kneeler there were flowers dedicated especially to the bride – bluebells from Scotland and snow gum from Tasmania.

The American reporter in the press box, who did not even recognise the bridegroom, had to surrender: 'This is better than the Oscars.'

Mary's stepmother, Susan Donaldson, was shown to her seat by her youngest son, Ben Moody. The royal couple made their entrance to the sound of Spanish music, the fanfare from 'Seis Conciertos de dos organos obligados' by Antonio Soler. The Crown Prince and his brother got kisses on the cheeks and a squeeze on the shoulders. By now the atmosphere in the church was electric. Only two seats were still empty. The bells of the cathedral rang out to proclaim the wedding.

Crown 1 had been back to Amalienborg to collect the bride and her father, and the black limousine was again getting close to Nørregade. Bridesmaids and page boys were ready to receive them. When the roar from the mass of people outside penetrated through to the Crown Prince and close to 700 guests in the church, the bridegroom found it hard to keep his composure. He breathed deeply, swallowed and blinked constantly. Time stood still; the chiming of the bells turned to the regular striking of the hour. She must be here soon. Even before the big porch doors opened, heavy tears fell down Frederik's cheeks. The Queen was almost as emotional as her son. At that moment she was not the sovereign, she was a mother.

The prelude to Händel's grandiose coronation hymn 'Zadok the Priest' struck up and slowly the doors opened. When the chorus joined in, the enchantingly lovely Mary stepped in to the church on her father's arm. Frederik looked as if he were going to faint. But when he locked eyes with Mary and found support, his smile returned. She was just as beautiful as everyone had expected, dressed in an impressively simply cut eggshell-coloured duchess satin wedding dress with an open, boat neckline, three-quarter sleeves and a 6-metre-long train. Designed by Uffe Frank, a well-known Danish designer who has his own studio in Milan, the dress was made up of panels that opened out to show sections of antique Irish lace. Mary's long, dark hair was combed tightly back and swept up, and she wore the 100-year-old bridal veil of the same Irish lace, which had been a present from Irish nuns to Queen Ingrid's mother.

All the people who meant anything in Mary's life were in the church. First and foremost, Frederik. But also the family from Scotland and from Australia, including friends all the way back to her school years in Tasmania. Perhaps she was unaware that they were following her every movement. Her fellow student from the University of Tasmania, Hamish Campbell, was sitting near the centre aisle and could almost touch the bride. Lawyer Matthew Annells, whom Mary has known since her Tasmanian days, was there. Her flatmate from Porter Street in Sydney, Andrew Miles, attended together with her schoolfriend Mandy Ellis from Taroona High. Kylie Jones, with whom Mary had shared a house in

Sydney, and for whom she herself had been bridesmaid in Sydney, was there with her husband, Anthony. Girlfriends from Sydney, Emma Turnbull and Sacha Hodgson were there, along with Sarah Bellenger, Mary's colleague from Belle Property. And of course Chris Meehan, the founder of Belle Property, who is a good friend of both Mary and Frederik.

Her best friend, Amber Petty, whom Mary met when she was working at the advertising agency MOJO Partners in Melbourne, was one of the chosen ones. She is a daily studio host at MTV in Australia, and she knows how to behave with confidence in front of the cameras. She was bridesmaid together with Mary's sisters, Jane and Patricia. The three women were dressed in gowns designed by Uffe Frank in three different shades of red that harmonised perfectly with the red tones of the floral decorations. All had their hair swept up in 60s-style buns. Mary had also three small flower girls: Jane's daughters, Erin, eight years old; Kate, six; and Patricia's eight-year-old daughter, Maddison. And she had two small page boys: Prince Joachim and Princess Alexandra's four-year-old son, Prince Nikolai, and his great-cousin, the four-year-old Count Richard, who is the son of Princess Alexandra and Count Jefferson. Bridesmaids and page boys adjusted Mary's long train and followed slowly behind the bride and her father.

John Donaldson was beaming with pride. Like his brother, brother-in-law and cousin, he was of course also dressed in a Scottish kilt. He walked with a wide, proud smile and with Mary's hand resting on his arm. Now was the moment when he would give his youngest daughter away under circumstances which he surely had never in his wildest dreams envisaged. He bowed to the royal couple and gave his future son-in-law a firm handshake, as if to say: 'Now she is yours, my son. Look after her well.'

At long last, the bride and groom stood together. They exchanged a soft kiss on the cheek and sat down in front of the altar on the bridal hassock, with upholstery embroidered by Queen Ingrid. They took each other by the hand and Mary beckoned to her bridesmaid, Amber, to take the bridal bouquet. Frederik looked enchanted at his bride and whispered words that only Mary could hear.

The bride sang along in Danish when the first hymn, 'The Blessed Day', rang out in the church. Mary had practised well. After a prayer and a reading by the bishop of the Copenhagen diocese, Erik Normann Svendsen, the next hymn was the powerful English 'Eternal Father', which was Mary's mother's favourite hymn. It had been sung at Henrietta Donaldson's funeral in 1997. The person with whom Mary would more than anyone else have wanted to share her happiness could not be present. During the third verse of the hymn, the thought of the loss of her mother became too much for Mary. Tears rolled down her cheeks, and she squeezed Frederik's hand. The TV cameras considerately avoided close-ups of the bride and groom.

Erik Normann Svendsen then addressed the bride and groom in a modern and personal speech that took as its starting point the overwhelming experience it must be for the bride to be followed by millions of TV viewers. 'Somehow, we all take part in your joy and happiness, as we follow the events of the day. Hence the great expectations towards this wedding – and therefore we all – big and small – take part in the joy. A royal couple does not belong solely to each other, but to all of us. We feel it, and you know it. Great assignments and many obligations await you, who will continue the Danish monarchy and thereby the Danish social structure. It is of crucial importance that this is maintained and renewed at a time marked by internationalisation and globalisation. Every monarch and every sovereign couple in Denmark has in the course of time contributed to the society we know and acknowledge today. That is why the monarchy is so firmly established with the Danish people.'

The bishop spoke direct to the bride: 'Dear Mary Donaldson! You have come to us from the far side of the earth. From the beautiful and mountainous Tasmania to the low-lying delightful Denmark. Both of our countries are characterised by the sea and the changing seasons. From today you are a real princess who has got both the prince and the entire kingdom. We can almost continue with the words of the fairytale: "And they lived happily ever after". But nothing in the real world is as un-complicated as the fairytales. We all know that from our own lives, and there is no reason to hide it. Joys and sorrows both belong to human life. That is why we need to be encouraged and comforted and to give comfort and encouragement to others. Living happily has less to do with feelings than with life succeeding in something good and fruitful. Thus, in spite of many encounters during the course of a lifetime, we are allowed to experi-ence life as meaningful, because we make a difference, primarily in close and binding commitments like marriage, friendship and relationships.'

After the Motet by Palestrina, which has been played at many church ceremonies in the royal family, the bishop nodded discreetly to the bride and groom. They rose and went up the four steps towards the altar. The moment had arrived.

'I now ask you, Frederik André Henrik Christian, will you take Mary Elizabeth Donaldson, who stands by your side, to be your wife?' A clear 'Yes' was heard throughout Vor Frue Kirke. 'And I ask you, Mary Elizabeth Donaldson, will you take Frederik André Henrik Christian, who stands by your side, to be your husband?' And of course the answer was yes, but the microphones revealed that Mary's voice was thick with emotion. The wedding and this magic moment was theirs alone. They shared it with each other and the bishop. No one else was party to it. The bride and groom had requested that the cameras let them have this holy moment in peace – no close-ups. Yet all the guests in the church and the millions of viewers felt that they were never closer to the couple than at this moment.

A few seconds later, the cameras had again found the bride and groom and the bishop: 'I now declare you married in the eyes of both God and man. In the name of the Father, the Son and the Holy Ghost. Amen.'

Mary Elizabeth Donaldson was now Her Royal Highness Crown Princess Mary Elizabeth. And she now had on her ring finger a wedding band of Greenland gold, simple and classical, made from the first gold that was mined in Greenland. The bride and groom have followed the Australian custom to wear the ring on the left hand rather than on the right, as is Danish tradition. And it was as if peace at long last had descended over the Crown Prince. When the newlyweds with their hands tightly entwined listened to the music of Palle Mikkelborg's 'A Simple Prayer', Frederik let out a sigh of relief and smiled lovingly at his wife.

After the traditional Danish wedding hymn 'It is so lovely to walk together', a prayer and the blessing by the Royal Chaplain, Christian Thodberg, the congregation sang 'Now Thank We All Our God'. And then, all of a sudden it was over. The Crown Prince and Princess stood up, the Crown Princess curtsied to the Queen, and the Queen responded with a fingertip kiss to her new daughter-in-law.

To the sounds of the virtuoso French organ symphony Toccata in F-major from Charles-Marie Widor's fifth organ symphony, the newlyweds slowly walked out of the cathedral. Happy, relieved and immensely in love. Mary looked with longing at her prince. Then, in a little break, while Mary's train was being adjusted, at long last, he gave his Crown Princess the kiss the whole of Denmark had been waiting for. Now was the right time for the public kiss. Frederik made the decision. And Mary had been waiting happily.

The cheering had no end when the Crown Prince and Princess stepped out from the cathedral. Thousands of Danes waving the Danish flag and Australian flag had waited for hours to catch a glimpse of the newlyweds, and exactly the moment they stepped out from the church, the sun broke through the clouds. Right to the last minute, the weather had been unpredictable and the court's stable manager waited till the last minute to confer with the Crown Prince to decide if the couple would drive in an open Barouche carriage through the streets of Copenhagen from the cathedral to Amalienborg. The carriage was drawn by six white horses and escorted by 48 royal guardsmen on horseback and in gala uniforms.

The Copenhagen police estimated that almost 100,000 people followed the coach through the streets of Copenhagen. On the way, there was entertainment for the married couple and for those waiting. At the Town Hall square, 120 choristers sang 'In Denmark I Was Born' for the newlyweds and at the memorial anchor in Nyhavn, in the old quarter of Copenhagen, the Danish Navy's drum corps played for them. More than 20,000 people gathered in the Amalienborg castle square. Many had waited since midmorning to get a good spot. 'Frederik and Mary, come outside, otherwise we'll never go home,' they chanted in time, in a 2004 version of the traditional call from the castle square. (Each year on Queen Margrethe's birthday the crowd yell out, 'Come out, come out, or we'll never go home' until their monarch makes her appearance on the balcony.)

At the stroke of six, the newlyweds stepped out on the balcony of Christian VII's palace. But there was a confidence and tranquillity which cannot be compared to the slightly frightened and overwhelmed expression Mary had in her eyes when five months earlier as a newly engaged woman she was cheered from the castle square. Now she was just happy and relieved. Frederik was bursting with pride whenever he looked at his bride. The cheers would not stop when they finally kissed each other.

After a few minutes, they were joined on the balcony by Queen Margrethe and Prince Henrik as well as John and Susan Donaldson. The Queen called for three cheers for the Crown Prince and Princess, and then the Royal Guard's Music Corps played the royal anthem, 'King Christian Stood at the Lofty Mast'.

The Crown Prince had a firm hold around the waist of his beautiful bride, and several times they exchanged hugs and kisses on the cheek. But not long, intense kisses. They are reserved for privacy. The Crown Prince and Princess have set clear and precise boundaries for what they want to share with others. Twice the couple came out on the balcony, and the band played 'Crown Prince Frederik's Salutation March' and, at Mary's request, 'Waltzing Matilda', which to many Danish ears is synonymous with the Australian national anthem.

The newlyweds were so overwhelmed by the cheers and outpouring of love from the crowd that it seemed they floated on a cloud of happiness, the breathless and exhausting pre-wedding program quite forgotten. In fact, the couple had been rushed off their feet for weeks, without anyone noticing any strain on them. The prelude to the wedding of the century had lasted for months, indeed, almost since the day of the engagement in October. Not only had Mary worked hard at learning her new homeland's language and studying Danish democracy while slowly starting to realise the extent of her new life's most challenging task, that of becoming a crown princess. She and Frederik had also been a part of the most minute details – the invitations, the seating plan for the dinner, the menu, but also the composition of the extensive program in the weeks leading up to the royal wedding.

It was not only Mary and Frederik who were getting married on 14 May. It seemed that the whole of Denmark was getting married along with them, and millions of Danes allowed themselves the pleasure of reflecting in the glory of the royal romance. Wedding coins and special stamps had been issued, money had been collected for a present from the people with which all Denmark could identify, and the newspapers polled the Danes about their attitude to the monarchy and to Mary. Mary had gone to the top of the class. The Danes had taken their future Crown Princess to their hearts; they trusted her, they saw how happy their Crown Prince was, and eight out of ten Danes told a Gallup opinion poll, published a few weeks prior to the wedding, that the monarchy was the right form of rule in Denmark. Never before had an opinion poll given the Danish royal family such a vote of support. Danish republicans may just as well pack their bags, because they are in the minority.

Mary has succeeded in simultaneously giving the monarchy a touch of magic, contemporary style and mysticism, while also being down to earth, popular, young and innovative. Even young intellectuals who like to call the royal family outdated and out of sync with the people have surrendered to the sporty, rock music-loving Crown Prince and Princess. They have united the nation across political attitudes, skin colour and age.

The defence forces paid tribute to the Crown Prince and Princess on the anniversary of the liberation of Denmark on 5 May with a parade of honour from the three services, the navy, the air force and the army, along with the Home Guard at Langelinie, right outside Mary's flat. Mary demonstrated her natural talent for her new role when she waved and smiled to the thousands of people who had come to the wharf, and she spent extra time waving to the many kindergarten children who had turned up to take part in the event. The defence force parade was also the starting signal for a tiring nine-day-long program, where Mary and Frederik to the delight of the people made themselves available so that as many as possible could take part in the wedding festivities.

Throughout the many diverse events, the young couple demonstrated that they fully understood that the Danish monarchy only exists as long as it has the support of the people; that it constantly has to prove its value and justify its existence by being a rallying point for the Danes. While others would faint from exhaustion after having the cameras rolling all the time and a couple of thousand media representatives from all around the world chasing them, Mary took it all in her stride. More than 40,000 Danes bought tickets to the concert 'Rock'n Royal' in the Parken in Copenhagen, where Danish and Australian bands entertained the crowd and the profits went to the aid organisation Red Barnet, of which the Crown Prince is a patron. On the Saturday, the Australian Governor-General, Michael Jeffery, invited Mary's family, the royal family and the Australian Ambassador in Denmark to a gala dinner at Fredensborg Store Kro on the occasion of the wedding. The famous inn lies a few hundred metres from Mary and Frederik's new premises, the Chancellery house at Fredensborg, and it was here that the whole of Mary's family and nephews and nieces had been staying in the week before the wedding.

Sunday was the day of a sailing match on Copenhagen harbour, where Frederik and Mary competed with a Danish and an Australian crew respectively. Mary won and was crowned 'Queen of the sea'. On Tuesday evening, three days before the wedding, Queen Margrethe invited Danish dignitaries to a gala dinner in the banquet hall at Christiansborg. For the first time, Mary wore the Order of the Elephant; the order that was worn by Frederik's beloved grandmother, Queen Ingrid. Mary has inherited Ingrid's regalia and the same evening the future crown princess also made her debut wearing a tiara and Queen Ingrid's ruby set which is part of the crown jewels held at Rosenborg castle.

When Mary – dressed in a light silver-grey brocade gown in princess style with train, a light blue sash with the elephant, rubies around her neck and the beautiful tiara in her hair – stepped into the banquet hall accompanied by the trumpet fanfares of the Guard's band, the assembly gasped in spite of the fact that they were among those who regularly mixed with royalty. In came a worthy future queen. Prime Minister Anders Fogh Rasmussen was the evening's main speaker and he emphasised the fact that Frederik and Mary have the ability to be a royal house of their time. With reference to Hans Christian Andersen's fairytale about the princess and the pea, he spoke directly to Mary:

'I don't know if the Crown Prince has exposed you to the pea test. But if he has, he would have come to a conclusion that is the opposite to the outcome of the story. The Crown Prince is a considered man, and he knows that in our time, a real princess must not be thin-skinned at all. On the contrary, a real modern princess must be rather thick-skinned,' the Prime Minister said, with reference to the massive media interest and colossal pressure of expectations from Danish royal-watchers.

The busy program also included official visits with presentations of wedding gifts both in the parliament and at Copenhagen Town Hall. There were several wedding rehearsals in the cathedral, and a party for the younger generation in the People's House, Vega, at Vesterbro in Copenhagen. It was a party that the Crown Prince and Princess insisted on having for themselves. There were no direct TV transmissions. It was a happy evening with their best friends and acquaintances from Denmark and Australia and many representatives from the Danish cultural scene, as well as the couple's young royal friends and cousins from Norway, Sweden and Greece.

In the Royal Theatre, the evening before the wedding, Mary and Frederik were unexpectedly seated in the royal box, as a special gesture by Queen Margrethe. The gala performance on the royal stage broke with tradition; for the first time a band was playing hip hop music on the historic stage. The music of youth was acknowledged as an art form and was on show to kings, queens, princes and princesses from all the European royal houses.

Mary, who was dressed in a red dress – the colour of love, with heart-shaped sleeves – looked out on the gala dressed assembly from the royal box. It was the last evening that she could call herself Mary Elizabeth Donaldson. The next evening she would be a royal in earnest, for ever and ever. In the royal box she was sitting upright, looking out over her family, her in-laws, her friends and representatives of Denmark's high offices. Perhaps as she gazed she experienced again the overwhelming feeling of the magnitude of her new life as a crown princess. So much in love, she squeezed Frederik's hand tenderly and looked both moved and reflective. Mary knew the dutiful role she was stepping into. She was aware of its seriousness and the responsibility it entailed, even as she enjoyed the opera, ballet and rock. For Mary, Frederik is her happiness, he is her love, here now and forever, and it is simple and straightforward to join with him in marriage and at the same time reconcile herself to her royal destiny. She had never aspired to notoriety, had never had ambitions about walking on the red carpet in stiletto heels while the flashlights blazed. All she had done was seek happiness, and he is by her side now. Happiness and life. So simple and so magic. The loneliness and insecurity had gone. For both Frederik and Mary their togetherness and confidence are unique. They enjoy being in love and are both impatiently looking forward to having children, many children; to create together a loving home filled with life and laughter.

'I have always known about happiness, because my father has always said again and again: "Do what makes you happy." That is the most important thing,' Mary said to Ninka in an interview in *Politiken*. 'Right now I can say it is a very happy time. Very happy for us, for my family and for Frederik and his family. Also for the Danes, who are interested in the royal family. At the same time, we know that for some young people we are a kind of role model, that we are looked upon as a kind of ideal. But my own role will first and foremost be that of a loving and loyal support, Frederik's confidante in all matters. Also a kind of ideas person, so we can work together on the task ahead, because I can show strength in relation to other people. He knows that he can trust me completely. My education and my background, like my sense of logic, can be of help. I also believe that I can open his eyes to other ideas and support him in exploring new possibilities. I don't know where the limit is for that support, but I am a person to be trusted. I am strong; I don't break down.'

Mary's close friends were also at the Royal Theatre, as they had been right from when the love affair in Sydney began. They were fascinated by the cobbled streets in Copenhagen, breathless over the hectic wedding program and wildly surprised at seeing their childhood friend, fellow student and colleague on the front pages of the newspapers and weekly magazines. Not in their wildest dreams had they imagined that the monarchy was so popular or that the new Crown Princess had received such a warm welcome and was already idolised.

'I'm dumbfounded,' said Mary's good friend Hamish Campbell, who like most of her thirtysomething Australian friends had set foot in Denmark for the first time.

Like Andrew Miles, Mary's good friend and flatmate from Porter Street in Sydney, and others, he stayed at the Royal Hotel in the centre of Copenhagen in the week leading up to the wedding. Mary is a thoughtful hostess; she personally recommended and planned outings around the capital and on the island of Zealand, so that her friends were able to get a good impression of her new homeland. And Mary also recommended a trip to Sweden across the Sound.

'It is a fantastic fairytale land, and we enjoy it. It is a big experience for

Mary attending the Danish Lutheran Church in Sydney, March 2005

Mary and Frederik with Governor-General Michael Jeffery and Marlena Jeffery
at Government House, Canberra, March 2005

Frederik trying to make a paper ship at the Nordic pavilion at the World Expo, Nagakute, Japan, April 2005

Mary helps to plant a tree at the Hans Christian Andersen park in
Funabashi, Japan, April 2005

us to attend a gala performance at the Royal Theatre and of course also to attend the solemn wedding ceremony at the cathedral,' says Hamish Campbell. At the party for the younger set at Vega he had a chance to say hello informally to many of Frederik and Mary's Danish friends, and he was very happy to see that Mary was her usual self: smiling, full of energy and not weighed down by the heavy media presence and her many official responsibilities.

'She is herself, with the integrity and down-to-earth outlook that have always been her trademarks. She seems secure and convincing in her new role, and it is lovely not only to see her so happy, but also to find her unchanged as a person,' says Hamish Campbell. He had last seen Mary in January 2004, when she was in Hobart for her sister Patricia's wedding and also spent a couple of days in Sydney. Hamish was on that occasion host for an informal welcome-home party for Frederik and Mary, and now his former fellow student Mary is wearing the Danish crown jewels and being photographed with a tiara in her hair. For all her friends, it is unreal to see practical Mary all of a sudden being a star.

Hamish Campbell had considered very seriously what his present to the bride and groom should be. 'I wanted to give them something personal, and so I chose a framed antique map of Van Diemen's Land, dated 1840,' he says. The antique map is one of the earliest made of Tasmania, which was settled by the British in 1830. And the first Dane who settled in Tasmania, the explorer Jørgen Jürgensen, has had an influence on the map. At the end of 1826, the Danish adventurer led the first expedition that traversed the island from north to south in order to map it. It wasn't possible to get a trained cartographer to do the job, but the convict Jørgen Jürgensen could both read and draw maps and was willing to risk his life to traverse the Tasmanian wilderness in the hope of being pardoned and regaining his freedom.

Jørgen Jürgensen, who has never played a significant role in Danish history, is enjoying a renaissance in Denmark, 201 years after he – certainly as the first Dane and among the first Europeans – set foot on Tasmanian soil. Both the Danish Prime Minister and the Crown Prince mentioned the Danish explorer in their wedding speeches to Mary.

In Denmark the wedding program went like clockwork, everything according to plan, but after the wedding and the couple's appearance on the balcony at Amalienborg the timetable slipped for the first time in the long wedding week. At twelve minutes past seven, after the official photographs at Amalienborg, the Crown Prince and Princess drove towards their much-anticipated wedding reception at Fredensborg castle. The last 600 metres of the ride to the castle took place in an open Landauer coach, drawn by four dark horses and escorted by riders from the local riding school. But the couple did not arrive at the steps of the castle until twenty minutes past eight. According to the plan, the guests should by then have started dinner. No definitive explanation for the delay was given. The police denied that demonstrations at the Triangle at Østerbro had delayed the bride and groom. The Crown Prince and Princess were not going that way at all. But everything, even delays, can be forgiven on Denmark's day of celebration. It is a family celebration, and things take the time they take, said the palace spokesperson, who had not wanted to force the tempo.

Some of the guests from the wedding ceremony in the cathedral had been culled. There simply was not enough room at Fredensborg, and so those guests had their wedding dinner at other venues in North Zealand. But about 400 people, the royal guests, Denmark's dignitaries and the closest friends of the host and the bride and groom were at the celebrations in the big marquee that had been erected in the garden behind the castle. Mandy Ellis, Sarah Bellenger, Sacha Hodgson, Kylie Jones and her husband, along with Hamish Campbell and Chris Meehan, were all at the dinner in the marquee with the Crown Prince and Princess.

The Royal Guard's Band played under the giant 1400 square metre marquee. The musicians had been busy all day. First the changing of the guard at Amalienborg at twelve noon, then the brass players at the wedding in the cathedral, and next the whole band entertained when the couple stepped out on the balcony at Amalienborg. Now they were sitting ready in the marquee at Fredensborg, where they were also to play. The musical program spoke of love and romance. Waldteufel's 'Amour et Printemps'; Grieg's 'Wedding Day at Troldhaugen'; H.C. Lumby's 'Amorin Polka'; 'One Hand, One Heart' from Leonard Bernstein's *West Side Story*. And especially for Mary, the conductor, Peter Harbeck, had put together a potpourri of Australian songs.

The colours of love were dominant here also. They were used in the flower arrangements which were dominated by sweet pea in the most beautiful shades of red, rose and pink.

Prince Henrik, as host, welcomed the guests from near and far in what he described as 'an ecstasy of happiness'. Then the prince addressed his daughter-in-law directly. 'There is no doubt that the shining star of this beautiful day is you, Mary, full of grace and charm. In finding the way to the heart of our beloved son Frederik, you have followed your own heart as well as your instinct. I have noticed from the first encounter with you, your reserve, your sense of duty that matches the strength and mastery of your feelings – these are important qualities in your coming life that opens its official gates to you on this happy day. Welcome to our family and to our hearts, where you will always find a warm refuge, if you need it.'

Of course the Crown Prince got some well-meaning words from papa. 'From a distant island you bring a fresh and lovely flower to grace our Danish isles. I know that you possess the qualities to make that flower thrive and flourish here with us,' said Prince Henrik among other things to his eldest son.

No one that evening doubted that Prince Henrik is enchanted by his lovely daughter-in-law. Perhaps he was also on this special day recalling his own feelings when, 37 years earlier, on 10 June 1967, he said yes to the heir to the throne, Margrethe, and in this place, under a marquee at Fredensborg, talked about his wife as 'the loveliest decoration of the garden'. They share something, Mary and Henrik: the experience of coming as a foreigner to Denmark and marrying the heir to the Danish throne. And the upheaval; to be all of a sudden part of a royal house with etiquette, protocol and centuries-old traditions.

For months the media had been guessing about the wedding dinner menu. Anything from Australian specialities, from emu and kangaroo to Tasmanian wine had been suggested. But it was the French-born Prince Henrik who was the man behind the culinary tribute to the bride and groom. And it was a dinner with equal inspiration from the French and the Danish kitchen. The first course was a timbale of shellfish from the Nordic seas: small shaped mounds of minced fish based on turbot with a ragout of shellfish such as Norwegian lobsters, scallops and freshwater shrimps. With this was served a sauce of sea urchin, a delicacy. The main meal consisted of roast venison from the royal forests, very likely hunted by Prince Henrik himself, and with that was served tender, new Samsø potatoes baked in puff pastry, peas, and morels, which are a type of spring mushroom. As a side dish there was a vol-au-vent named 'Perfect Union' in reference both to its delicate mingling of flavours of chicken, asparagus and apple cider and the anticipated happy relationship between Frederik and Mary. The dessert was a cake of white chocolate mousse, dedicated to the

Crown Prince and Princess. The wines were from Prince Henrik's French wine estate castle, Château de Caïx; the champagne was from the house of Mercier. It was a special bottling, dedicated to the couple – Champagne Mercier Cuvée Frederik & Mary.

After the first course, the Queen spoke, and it was first and foremost as a mother that she addressed her eldest son. 'You have a warm heart which strikes everyone who meets you. You inspire confidence. You are a person to rely on. Much of this is the result of your own efforts. However, we your parents, Papa and Mother, know very well how you have found your true self. That happened when you met Mary. It brought springtime into your heart and everything blossomed around you, as we see season in full bloom on this day in May.' On behalf of the whole country and directly addressing the new Crown Princess, the Queen welcomed Mary: 'Mary, today all Denmark welcomes you with open arms, and your new family welcomes you with great joy. We have come to know you and we have seen how your cheerful disposition graces your every act. You have met us, your new family and all your new countrymen with warmth and great dignity. You too inspire confidence, around you too the Garden of Denmark is decked with flowers.'

The Queen also used her speech to remember two people who had not lived to experience Frederik and Mary's happy day as bride and groom and who were painfully missed: Queen Ingrid and Mary's mother, Henrietta. 'Mr Donaldson, this day is a celebration for all of us. But for you and your family it is not without a note of sadness, for one person is greatly missed – Mary's mother, who we in Denmark shall never know, but who should have been at her daughter's side on this day of happiness.'

And surprisingly, the Queen praised Mary for the courage she had shown in choosing to make her future life in Denmark: 'She has great inner strength, and she exudes a calm warmth that inspires confidence. She has shown the courage to place her future life in Denmark. May we always be worthy of her trust. The Prince Consort and I welcome her into our family and into her new country.'

It is a tradition for the bride's father to make a speech, and John Donaldson gave a liberatingly straightforward address, which would have been well received by any good family, but which also made an impression on the many crowned heads at the party. John Donaldson would no doubt have been a happy and satisfied father, no matter which background his new son-in-law had had. But there is no doubt that he feels especially proud about giving his daughter away to a prince. And yet, the humorous Scot could not resist teasing his new Danish family. 'In the twelfth century, the marauding Vikings were driven out of Scotland after much savage fighting by a band of men led by the grandfather of the first Donald, the founder of the clan MacDonald. He would have wondered why he went to so much trouble when, some eight centuries later, we take account of today's union between the Viking Frederik and Mary of the MacDonald clan.'

John Donaldson reflected with love on his late wife, Henrietta, who 'would have been so happy for Mary on this her special day.' And the speech was, against custom at these sort of occasions, interrupted by spontaneous applause, when he declared that he was the proud father of a loving daughter. Everybody present agreed.

The Crown Prince's new father-in-law bid Frederik welcome to the family, and there was no doubt that Frederik had settled very well into his new family.

The Crown Prince started the speech of his life with a thankyou to his father-in-law. 'One might say that Mary also belongs to you – but as of today she belongs to me – and I belong to her.' Spontaneous laughter and applause interrupted him for a short time before he continued, assuring his father-in-law that he would protect Mary and do everything to make her feel secure and at home in her new homeland.

Rarely has the Crown Prince been more calm and spoken more compellingly than when he thanked the love of his life. He talked with raw honesty about how lonely and searching he had been before on only his second day in Australia he fell for Mary's beauty and charisma, and their fates had been sealed. 'Your radiance shone clearly for me from our very first meeting. Since then, I have been blinded by it and totally dependent on it.'

The Crown Prince can't get enough of his lovely Crown Princess, and he hungers to know what life has to offer them, what they will experience and learn together. 'I am almost bubbling over with curiosity as to what the near and distant future has in store for us – and it is you who must answer. But I will try to control myself for two questions have already been answered with a simple "Yes" from us both. It is an answer that will hold good for us always. And if we need light in our search for answers, all we need to do is to lift our eyes and look towards heaven. There lies eternity, which can always show us the way back to the path we sometimes lose.'

And with words borrowed from his friend, Danish rock musician, Lars H.U.G., Frederik declared his great love for Mary: 'I love you, Mary. Come, let us go! Come, let us see! Throughout a thousand worlds, weightless love awaits.' Mary's eyes glimmered. That sentence means something quite special for the two of them.

More than several weeks' wedding celebrations had almost come to an end. Soon they could party freely with family and friends, soon they could get out of uniform and bridal gown, put on some casual clothes and take off for the honeymoon. One last thing was to come, and they got there in time, before the bell struck twelve. In the domed hall, where so many before them have danced on the star-patterned, black-and-white marble floor, Frederik and Mary stepped out for the big finale. To Niels W. Gade's music for August Bournonville's 'A Folk Tale' the couple moved carefully, warmly, tenderly on the floor to the bridal waltz. Perhaps they would not have been given top marks for technique but, on the other hand, they would have scored maximum for artistic and emotional expression. Love had joined two continents. The Crown Prince had found his princess; the girl from Tasmania had found her prince.

Chapter 10

MARY MANIA

'Denmark is my home, but it's good to be back in Australia.' Ten months after her wedding to Crown Prince Frederik, the transformation from Australian businesswoman to Danish crown princess is a reality, and in flawless Danish, Crown Princess Mary answers the Danish journalists who have followed the Crown Prince and Princess on their first official visit to Mary's country of birth.

The visit to Australia completed the circle; even though Mary misses her friends and her family, she is now Danish. She behaves so naturally as a crown princess that many forget she was not born into royalty. Mary is very much present when she represents Denmark and it is hard to recall that she has not always been the focal point. She walks, waves, receives flowers and converses with ease. She presents herself with elegance and naturalness, as if it is quite normal that curious eyes should follow her every move and capture it all on camera.

And of course Mary took her old homeland by storm when she and the Crown Prince began their official visit to Australia at the end of February 2005. As it happened, Prince Charles was also visiting Australia at this time. But it was 'Our Princess', as the newspapers named her, who was running away with all the attention. Even if Mary is a Danish crown princess, she is also Australia's princess, and the Australians love her. Forget about surfing and jogging – Sydney's new favourite sport is princess-spotting.

Opinion pollsters Media Monitors noted that the Crown Prince and Princess's visit was reported no less than 7272 times in the Australian media. Mary and Frederik attended four charity dinners in Sydney, for, among others, Red Cross, cancer research and mental illness, and the total income from the ticket sales added up to close to $2.15 million (10 million kroner). When former American president Bill Clinton visited Sydney last, he was followed closely by 50 journalists. One hundred and thirty members of the media followed Mary's debut on the Australian scene.

The Danish Consul General in Sydney, Jørgen Møllegård, was deeply involved in the planning and execution of the royal visit. And he gives Mary top marks:

'The mark for the Crown Princess's effort is ten out of ten. She was clearly impressed by the incredibly positive reception in the press and from people who came to see her. She has taken the Australians by storm, among other things by accepting the many flower bouquets, which children especially were carrying as they stood along the route. Often she went outside the roped-off areas to say hello to some schoolchildren.' In Møllegård's opinion, there was not a note of criticism from the Australians, 'they are simply so proud of her. At the many dinners and receptions she conversed animatedly with high and low, and everywhere she presented herself in the most beautiful manner,' he says.

Even though the visit to Australia was packed with official duties, Mary also took time to see her friends with whom she has been in contact by telephone and email from Denmark. She spent her only free day in

Sydney with her best friend and bridesmaid Amber Petty. And her old friend and fellow student from Tasmania, Hamish Campbell, was on hand to help Mary when the interest of the press got a bit too intrusive – just as he had been when the media first got wind of the romance between the dark-haired girl from Belle Property and the Crown Prince from the far north. Hamish simply came to the rescue of Mary and Amber in a yacht, picking them up from the Pier Restaurant at Rose Bay and taking them to safety away from the curious media. And when Mary and the Crown Prince were sailing against each other in a race on Sydney Harbour, she also got a chance to renew old friendships. It was the couple's good friend, Mary's former boss from Belle Property, Chris Meehan, who skippered Mary's boat.

After the first day's official duties, a few critical voices emerged. First and foremost they came from the Danish media, who thought that Mary was much more relaxed and spontaneous when she was in Denmark. In Australia, Mary and the Crown Prince were accused of surrounding them-selves with the elite. But Mary and her minders listened to the critics, and the Crown Princess began to take time to break her planned walks. She crouched down, shook hands, chatted and accepted drawings and flowers from little boys and princesses-to-be. And there was not a dry eye to be seen when Mary read Hans Christian Andersen's 'The Ugly Duckling' to sick children at Sydney's Westmead Children's Hospital.

Celebrations to mark the two-hundredth anniversary of the birth of Hans Christian Andersen were a substantial part of the visit, and the Crown Prince and Princess took the opportunity to appoint Hans Christian Andersen ambassadors. Mary became an honorary ambassador and Frederik stressed that his wife had in fact never been exposed to the 'pea test', as some have hinted at.

'I have talked to my mother about this, but there was no pea,' the Crown Prince relates. 'But if there was a pea, it certainly wasn't big enough to prevent the Crown Princess from meeting and succeeding in the challenges she has faced in our journey together so far.'

The Crown Prince and Princess had a wonderful secret during their official visit to Australia. Mary was in the early stages of her pregnancy. Only six to seven weeks pregnant, it was easy for Mary to hide her joyful news. And Frederik and Mary wanted to keep the news secret until they returned to Denmark. The couple who are so much in love wanted to enjoy their happy knowledge in peace for a little longer – there would be time enough to share it with a curious public. They would have to wait. But oh, how she was looking forward it, how both of them were looking forward to it, and how difficult it was not to show their elation to the world.

The quietly bubbling happiness at the thought of parenthood grew when Mary saw her eight Tasmanian nephews and nieces again. Mary's three siblings all have children, and Mary is quietly joyful soon she, too, will experience the miracle of being a mother. The next time she visits her home country, she will have a baby in her arms. The next time Mary visits Hobart, she can tell her child that her grandmother once went with her to this beach and that just here she played with the cat on the lawn, and then there was the time when grandad taught her to cycle without training wheels on the steep hill of her childhood street, Morris Avenue. But no one in Australia had guessed that Mary was pregnant and that in October she will give birth to a little prince or princess, an heir to the oldest royal house in the world. They didn't guess it at home in Tasmania where her visit was causing a media frenzy, although there was great speculation when Mary bought a pair of bootees in a Hobart shop. The day before the Crown Prince and Princess were due to arrive in Tasmania, the *Mercury* cleared the whole front page for a picture of Mary under the headline 'Mary

Mania'. And on the day the Crown Prince and Princess arrived on the island, the *Mercury*'s headline read 'Welcome home, Mary', printed on a royal blue background.

The return to the island of her birth made a deep impression on Mary. 'It is a strong feeling to return home. You remember all the things from your childhood. I thought very much of my mother,' Mary said. 'It was a beautiful feeling to see Tasmania below me and coming in to land because it is my home – my first home – you could say.' Officially, Denmark is her home now, but Tasmania will always be in her heart.

Before they left for Australia, Mary and Frederik disclosed that they had a secret dream of owning their own place in Tasmania. 'It would be wonderful to own a small piece of Tasmania,' said the Crown Princess to the *Mercury*, to whom she also disclosed that when the couple have children they will take them to Australia on a regular basis. 'I think it must be important for them to have a feeling for and an understanding of where I come from.'

Thousands of Tasmanians received the couple when they arrived on the island. Danish-born Inger-Lise Goyne lives in Hobart and has known Mary ever since she was a little girl, because her son and Mary's brother, John, were childhood friends. And Inger-Lise Goyne was part of the chorus of welcome.

'Tasmanians are wildly proud of Mary. They are overwhelmed and enthusiastic because Mary is handling her role as crown princess so impressively. The scepticism and indifference that surrounded Mary's relationship with a faraway crown prince in the beginning is completely gone and has been replaced by pride. Now Tasmanians are mad about her and everybody is happy for her,' says Inger-Lise Goyne, who with about 1000 others was invited to the reception for the Crown Prince and Princess at Hobart's finest hotel, Wrest Point.

Yet, the accolades in Tasmania were more subdued than in the rest of Australia. Tasmanians are proud of 'Our Mary', but by nature are perhaps a little more reticent to display their feelings. But there's no doubt that they are proud of her, not least because she's so natural and unaffected.

'Mary has star quality, and at the same time she does not put on airs and graces, but has a sweetness about her, which by and large is very Tasmanian. That's why they love her in Hobart,' says Inger-Lise Goyne.

A commentary in one of the national papers even dared to claim that Mary will not be subject to the Australian counterpart to the Danish 'Law of Jante', the tall poppy syndrome, as long as she continues to look enchanting, quickly produces an heir and continues to look happy in the company of Frederik.

Mary's stepmother, the author Susan Donaldson, knows more than anyone how much the visit to Australia meant to Mary. Without doubt it is extremely important to Mary to be accepted on her home turf. 'It means a lot for Mary to be a success in Australia. She has made a great effort,' says Susan Donaldson.

She made an interesting observation during Mary's triumphant tour of Australia. 'The Australians imagine themselves as republicans and against royalty. And yet, they worship Mary and Frederik, and that is a paradox. That is a credit to Mary more than anything, because during her tour home where she had to prove to her countrymen that she is worthy of the title of Crown Princess, she has not set a foot wrong,' Susan says with conviction.

And Mary came close to converting some Australians sceptical of royalty. The *Sydney Morning Herald* carried out its own poll among 6450 of its readers. One-fifth said that they had become more royalist on account of Mary, although 58 per cent maintained that they were against the monarchy as an institution.

Federal health minister, Tony Abbott, thanked Mary for reminding a sceptical world of the magic which can be found in the monarchy. 'Every time a person's dreams come true, the world becomes a better place for us all. Your marriage is a gift to the people of Australia,' the *Sydney Telegraph* wrote.

Australians love a royal 'who is among us, not above us', as one newspaper put it. Mary is popular because Australians can identify with her. And Mary's favourite Australian sweets, Fruit Tingles – which are well known to all Australians – became a symbol of this identification. 'Charles has no real claim to being an Australian, and we feel no connection to him,' the *Sydney Morning Herald* wrote.

But not everyone was charmed. 'I have no intention of letting myself be carried away by royal fever. I don't even know how to curtsy,' said Senator Bob Brown from the Greens.

When the official visit was almost over, one journalist dared to ask a question that was considered improper by the royals. 'What do you think of Australia as a republic?' It was a question that Mary just a few years back would probably have had a clear position on. But before she had a chance to open her mouth, Crown Prince Frederik deftly deflected the question. 'That is a political question, which lies far from our area of responsibility.' Private opinions must stay private, and Mary knows this.

There are great expectations for the long-term effect of the royal couple's visit. 'The importance for Danish–Australian relationships, all things being equal, is enormous. During the royal couple's stay, we have had a press coverage which very few have had,' said the Danish Consul General in Sydney, Jørgen Møllegård.

He added, 'Denmark is known in every corner of Australia. Leading politicians, leading businesspeople, leaders of organisations and so on have been ready to sell their own grandmother for an invitation to the many functions that have been held during the royal visit.'

After the visit, Australians gave a sigh of relief. 'Drop the tiara,

Sydney is a princess-free zone,' one of the city's newspapers wrote, when the royal visit was over and Mary was looking forward to donning a pair of jeans and relaxing with Frederik, her father and Susan, her siblings and their families, and enjoying a private vacation after the official visit.

Mary misses her family. But she has her father within reach. John Donaldson and his wife, Susan, spend a few months each year in the city of Aarhus, where John Donaldson has been given a visiting professorship in mathematics at the university. Susan Donaldson, who still writes under her former name, Susan Moody, enjoys living in Aarhus, only a few minutes by bicycle from Marselisborg castle. There is nature, city life and the peace to work on her novels.

'We love living in Denmark. The Danes are sweet and hospitable. We enjoy living in Aarhus, because the town is small enough for us to quickly get to know it and at the same time big enough for us to have our private life. There is the loveliest view over the sea, and with the new art museum, Aros, the Old Town and all the historic museums, it is a gift to live in and explore Aarhus. We love to go on trips to the town of Ebeltoft, which is very beautiful,' says Susan Donaldson.

Mary appreciates having her father and stepmother close by a couple of months a year, and she has noticed that Susan Moody's romantic novels shoot up the Danish bestseller lists. The Danes are mad about anything that is connected to Mary, and no doubt the sales figures benefit from this.

Mary soon became a cover girl in Danish and Australian magazines, both the popular weeklies and the glossy monthly magazines. The photogenic and fashion-conscious Crown Princess posed in stunning gowns, displaying an easy elegance and a model's figure.

The weekly magazines in Denmark reached record distribution when the Crown Princess was on the cover and in Australia *Vogue* sold out in no

Mary with Thai dancers on her visit to tsunami-affected villages,
Khao Lak, Thailand, April 2005

Mary and Frederik during the Hans Christian Andersen
bicentenary celebrations, Copenhagen, April 2005

Mary performing her duties as High Patron of Science Day,
Helsingor, Denmark, May 2005

Mary and Frederik attending the ballet at the
Copenhagen Royal Theatre, June 2005

time when a regally elegant Mary appeared on its cover. Her media magnetism also meant that she has featured on the cover of German and Swedish magazines, and the readers of the British magazine *Hello!* elected her as the most elegant woman in 2004. Mary has boosted business for the weekly magazines, which ended the year 2004 with big profits because stories of a royal wedding and photos of a smiling Crown Princess sold beyond their expectations.

The media's constant attention wasn't only positive, though. In November, *Ekstra Bladet*'s front page carried accusations that Mary was lazy and taking too much time off. Six months after the wedding to Frederik the royal-critical tabloid took stock of the career of the Crown Princess, and the newspaper was not impressed. Mary was spending too much time on horses, shopping and fashion shows and although she was regarded as being a lovely clothes-horse, she was criticised for not taking on patronages for charitable organisations.

It was exactly that kind of aggressive curiosity from the press that Mary had given a lot of thought to before she said yes to Frederik and the title of Crown Princess. Mary may be annoyed over an unfair attack by the press, but she is not able to answer back. Such accusations can only be met with silence, no matter how unreasonable they may be, such as when shortly before Mary and Frederik's return trip to Australia *Ekstra Bladet* proclaimed on its front page that 'Mary kept quiet about affair'. There was no secrecy about the brief encounter with an Australian footballer a couple of months before she met Frederik, yet the newspaper had to cast suspicion on the brief flirtation. Mary has already learned the lesson about critical press stories: that they are soon forgotten. Still, the bad stories frustrate her.

But she laughed at the press when they constantly zoomed in on the royal stomach. Was the Crown Princess pregnant? Was she too thin? Was her stomach getting rounder? The Danes laid bets on whether she would be pregnant before Christmas or before the first wedding anniversary. When *Se og Hør* in the early part of the northern autumn of 2004 revealed that Mary had undergone ultrasound scanning at the state hospital in Copenhagen, the news echoed throughout the realm. The general opinion was that an ultrasound of her abdomen was a clear indication that the Crown Princess was pregnant. No doubt it was an expression of national wishful thinking that the Crown Princess would soon give birth to an heir to the throne. But the royal court ignored the rumours and kept silent.

The truth was revealed several weeks later. For months, the Crown Princess had suffered from painful gallstones and that was the reason for the now-famous ultrasound. She was operated on in secret and had her gall bladder removed by keyhole surgery. 'Birth to a gallstone,' was the cheerfully ironic headline in the newspapers. Later on, Mary related to journalist Andrew Denton on ABC TV's *Enough Rope* program that she had laughed at the newspapers' fanciful scribbling.

In addition to the Lord Chamberlain, Per Thornit, with whom she has a close and confidential relationship, Mary has a trusted group of professionals who have helped her adjust to her new public role and have ensured that her encounters with the media are positive and successful. She is surrounded all the time by her indispensable trio, who support her professionally and can take much credit for Mary's rapid adjustment to her new role. They are her hairdresser, Søren Hedegaard, stylist, Anja Alajdi, Neitzel and lady-in-waiting, Victoria Bernstorff-Gyldensteen. The royal house's new press officer, Lis M. Frederiksen, also advises Mary on how to behave in connection with interviews.

It was a hectic premiere year as Crown Princess. There was not much that the newly married couple was allowed to keep for themselves. But Mary and Frederik were left alone on their honeymoon. Frederik had planned it all as a surprise for Mary, and it was. Three weeks in Africa, south of the equator with safaris, camping, the grandeurs of nature and animal life, Africa's beautiful colours and unbelievable starry sky. The precise destination remained a well-kept secret from the curious Danes and Australians.

Besides the honeymoon and the Australian tour, an absolute highlight was the visit to Greenland. Mary had never been there before, but Frederik had told her about it on numerous occasions. Mary was at last introduced to the country that has left a deep and indelible impression on her husband.

'The people, the ice, the mountains – and the light, which is so colourful and which is ever changing. Greenland is overwhelming. In a way, I think it's rather nice that people don't know too much about Greenland. Many say that Tasmania, where I come from, is a very boring place. We keep it a secret that there are so many beautiful places – in that way we are protecting it. Greenland must remain a bit of a secret. No one must know everything, then the mystery disappears,' Mary enthused in Greenland's Tourist Board's paper, *Greenland Now*.

The official reason for the visit was the twenty-fifth anniversary of home rule in Greenland, and Queen Margrethe and Prince Henrik accompanied the Crown Prince and Princess on part of the tour. But the Crown Princess was also introduced to the northernmost part of the Danish realm and the people and environment that have captivated the Crown Prince.

Her visit to Greenland gave her food for thought. 'I think the whole world could learn to appreciate the simple things in life. There are so many things we so-called modern human beings fight for, which don't mean anything at all. We live such hectic daily lives today and we're always looking for more time. It is probably the same in Nuuk, but when you visit the small villages, it is the seasons that are their time manager … We can learn something from that.'

To great cheers, Mary wore the Greenland national costume twice during the visit – the pearl-embroidered costume that Greenland women had made for her as a wedding gift from the Greenland government. In two weeks, the couple visited towns and settlements from Narsarsuaq in the south to Qaanaaq in the north. In Qaanaaq Mary realised in earnest the deep impression that Greenland and the Greenlanders had made on Frederik, and when Frederik's old friends in the town greeted the couple with drum dancing, the tough expeditioner and sledge driver Frederik again shed tears.

In Qaanaaq, Frederik and Mary opened a new drop-in centre for the town's youth. To care for those who are disadvantaged is important for Frederik and Mary. When they arrived home they decided that a considerable part of the profit from the royal pre-wedding concert would now be directed to the new drop-in centre for disadvantaged children in Nuuk.

At the end of July, the royal summer cruise on *Dannebrog* commenced. The royal yacht visited the major ports of Aarhus, Ålborg, Sønderborg and Odense, where the Danes cheered Mary as though she were already their queen. Now the Danes in the north of Jutland, on the island of Funen, in the southern part of Jutland and the inhabitants of Aarhus had the chance to wave, cheer, present flowers and shake hands with the Crown Prince and Princess. It became more of a victory cruise than a summer cruise. Mary charmed everybody with her straightforward manner. Mary's 'Tassie ego' suits the Danish people to a tee, and during the summer cruise she showed the Danes that she is unaffected, unceremonious, stylish and elegant at the same time.

The jet set image that some people in provincial towns had ascribed to Mary was soon put to shame. Besides winning the popular vote by showing an interest for and engagement in the arts, music and history of her new homeland, Mary is loved by the Danes for a completely different reason.

She has evoked the sensitive side of Frederik, and the Danes worship her for that. And that explains to a great extent why the Danes, who are otherwise rather suspicious of outsiders, accepted the Australian Mary at once.

During the summer cruise, the royal couple also demonstrated that they are setting the scene for a less formal, and more youthful style than Queen Margrethe's. In Aarhus the summer cruise was transformed into a rock festival in the city's park when thousands of people from central Jutland rocked with the couple and were served fried kangaroo meat and Australian red wine.

At the same time, Mary and Frederik showed that they have a social conscience when, during a visit to Hans Christian Andersen's birthplace in Odense, in the midst of their busy program they spent a couple of hours in the socially underprivileged neighbourhood of Vollsmose. Eighty different nationalities live side by side in Vollsmose, and many children grow up in families where both father and mother are unemployed. The royal visit meant a lot to Vollsmose, and Mary and Frederik said hello and chatted to the children, who performed in a circus and did acrobatics on bicycles. Mary also took time to taste and compliment the neighbourhood mothers on their homemade Arabian falafel and sambusa, a kind of sweet cake.

Four years after their first meeting at the Olympic Games in Sydney, the couple visited Athens, where they followed all sports with enthusiasm. They cheered when the Danish women's handball team met South Korea in the finals and after a nerve-racking match won Olympic gold. The Australian athletes also had a visit from Mary, and she followed their efforts in swimming, sailing and athletics.

In the middle of September 2004, Queen Margrethe's Lord Chamberlain, Ove Ullerup, called a press conference in the Yellow palace near

Amalienborg. It is unusual for the court to call a press conference with a few hours' notice. Speculations abounded with hope and expectation that Mary was pregnant. But no, the occasion was not a happy event, but something as rare as a royal divorce. The marriage between Prince Joachim and Princess Alexandra was over. For a while, the royal idyll seemed to be cracking. The decision had been made for many months, but the strategy of the court had been to wait until the Crown Prince's wedding, the trip to Greenland and the summer cruise were well out of the way. Princess Alexandra has now bought a luxury villa in Copenhagen where she lives with her two sons. Joachim lives at Schackenborg castle in South Jutland.

Mary and Frederik had known about the marital problems for a long time and had kept quiet. In the middle of their great love affair, it had been hard to see the love between Joachim and Alexandra being ground down to nothing. And it was especially hurtful to know that Felix and Nikolai would become children of a broken home. But private life is sacrosanct, and not once did Mary and Frederik comment on the divorce in public.

The Crown Prince couple did not have much time to enjoy their home at Fredensborg. There were new events and new speeches to prepare. The two-hundredth anniversary of Hans Christian Andersen's birth has meant that in 2005 the Crown Prince and Princess have visited New York, London and Berlin to appoint Hans Christian Andersen ambassadors. In New York, Mary and Frederik visited a school for children in Harlem, and once more Mary showed her intuitive rapport with children, reading fairytales and clearly enjoying being part of their world.

Many, many Danish organisations approach the Danish court seeking Mary as their patron. But Mary does not say yes to just anything, and she insists on going through all the applications carefully herself, before she makes a decision. Mary long ago realised that haste makes waste when it comes to choosing a patronage for life. After consultation with Frederik in particular, along with her mother-in-law and Per Thornit, Mary will decide for herself. A kind of sceptical impatience emerged during the northern autumn – when would Crown Princess Mary come into her own, what does she want other than horses and fashion?

'She wants to make a difference and use the platform that the title of Crown Princess gives her to create a better life for others. That's why Mary is very concerned about choosing the right thing, which must be something she burns for with all her heart,' says Susan Donaldson. Mary's choice falls on the wellbeing of children, health, and combating of illness. Fashion is also on the list. So far she has taken on half a dozen patronages, but more will come as the Crown Princess looks through the stack of applications.

The Heart Foundation, which performs great work in the area of research into heart disease, is close to Mary because she lost her own mother after a heart operation. Mary never got the chance to say goodbye properly to her mother because she was taken from the family so suddenly, but through personal engagement she can raise the profile of research into heart disease. Her efforts may help more people to a better and longer life even if they suffer from heart problems.

In addition, Mary has become the patron for organisations such as the Danish Refugee Council, the National Association for Brain Damage, and the Danish Association for Mental Health, which works to support the mentally ill and their relatives. The Christmas Seal Foundation, which, among other things, works to help obese children, will also benefit from Mary's input. And finally, the fashion-conscious Mary has said yes to becoming patron for the Copenhagen International Fashion Fair and the Designers' Nest, which promotes young Danish designers.

Mary is on her way to establishing her role as a royal patron, and she will grow in the role, Susan Donaldson says. 'We can both feel and see that

Mary is happy. Yes, more than happy. She is comfortable with being a crown princess, and she knew quite well that when she married Frederik she married a country and a job for life at the same time. Look at her – she enjoys being with Frederik, and is also thriving in her job. Mary took her time and weighed everything up, but when she decided to say yes to Frederik and Denmark, she knew the duties and challenges she was in for – and she knew that she could cope. Otherwise she would have said no,' says Susan.

And during the press conference in Hobart after her successful Australian tour, Mary herself stressed that her life as a princess is not just romantic, idyllic and a life of idleness. 'Our life is real,' says Mary. Reality is not just red carpets, expensive clothes and stiletto heels. It consists of Danish lessons, planning state visits, speeches, protocol, etiquette and onerous official duties. Mary has realised that there must be much organisation and preparation behind the scenes, if she is to succeed as a royal.

Both friends and family form a close and inviolable ring around Mary, just as they did when her fantastic romance with Frederik began. She chooses her circle very carefully, because they clam up like oysters. They take part in protecting the royal mystique that surrounds Mary.

The love between Mary and Frederik has brought the King to the surface in Frederik. Pure and simple. Time after time, the Danes have elected Frederik Dane of the Year. They love him, but for years their love for the Crown Prince has been mixed with worry, because Frederik appeared restless, rootless, out of sorts and uneasy with his role as heir to the throne and the constant demands that the role would place on him. But for the first time, with Mary by his side, the Danes see a happy crown prince.

The Danes adore Mary as much as they do Frederik. Even republican Australians love Mary. Mary is a hit, a fashion icon, a princess with heart and style, and a crown princess in the absolute super league. But first and foremost, she is Mary.

The sailor and the navy frogman has reached his secure harbour. The Crown Prince is going to be a father, and both Frederik and Mary are looking forward to a big family, with lots of fun, laughter, love and life. When Frederik was a child, he and his brother Joachim very seldom had their meals with Queen Margrethe and Prince Henrik. The nannies provided a safe base in Frederik's childhood while his parents ruled the kingdom. Frederik does not want to expose his own children to this kind of strict upbringing, and Mary decided long ago that her children are not going to be looked after by nannies, but by mum and dad. A mother's heart beats in Mary. A father's heart beats in Frederik.

Chapter 11

THE WEDDING ALBUM

THE GOWN OF LOVE

With a secure sense of style, Crown Princess Mary assisted in designing her dream gown, the dress of life and love. In close cooperation with the Milano designer Uffe Frank, born in Skanderborg in Denmark and trained under Queen Margrethe's preferred fashion designer, Jørgen Bender, Mary had been a part of creating a wedding dress in white duchess satin that shines like mother-of-pearl.

Feminine, classical, modern and majestic. A masterpiece of a bridal dress. Sewn in long panels, which open out 10 centimetres below the waist to reveal the century-old lace that, like Mary's veil, originates from the nuns in Connaught in Ireland. The duchess satin shines like mother-of-pearl and is in close colour harmony with the old lace.

The designer, Uffe Frank, calls the sleeves 'kala' sleeves, because they fold themselves around the arms like the kala lily. Eight metres of the old lace was used for the dress as well as 24 metres of duchess satin, and the dress was lined with silk organza. In the silk organza of the skirt, light blue silk bows were hidden in keeping with the tradition that the bride must wear something blue. Twenty-three metres of duchess satin were used for the impressive train. It measured 6 metres from the waist, and it could be removed to allow the bride to dance the bridal waltz.

The veil of Irish lace was, together with lace edgings, a handkerchief and a fan, a present to Queen Ingrid's mother, Crown Princess Margret of Sweden, who used the veil and the lace at her wedding in St George's Chapel in Windsor on 15 June 1905. Queen Ingrid inherited the veil when her mother died. It was left with Queen Ingrid's mother in her coffin as she lay in state, but removed immediately before the funeral.

Queen Ingrid's three daughters have all worn the veil at their own weddings. Queen Anne-Marie wore the veil and the smaller pieces of lace on her dress for her wedding in Athens to King Konstantin II of Greece in September 1964, and Queen Margrethe used the veil and the wider pieces of lace on her dress at her wedding in the Holmen's Church in June 1967. Princess Benedikte used the veil and the wider pieces of lace on her dress at her wedding in Fredensborg castle's church in February 1968. And Princess Benedikte's daughter, Princess Alexandra zu Sayn-Wittgenstein-Berleburg, and Queen Anne-Marie's daughter, Princess Alexia of Greece, wore the historic veil at their weddings in the summers of 1998 and 1999 respectively. Mary is the first woman who is not a direct descendant of Queen Ingrid who has been allowed to wear the bridal veil – yet another gracious gesture towards the new Crown Princess.

The silk in the Crown Princess's bridal dress originates from the Chinese province of Zhejiang. In 2003, 200,000 silk cocoons of the finest quality were harvested for the dress. The thread from which the silk was spun was so long that it could in theory reach several times around the earth. The silk thread was sent to Bangalore in India where it was dyed in an ivory shade, close to the colour of the lace veil that Queen Ingrid had inherited from her mother.

The tailor, Birgit Hallstein, spent more than 300 hours with needle and thread in a specially fitted dressmaker's workroom at Amalienborg. Here, the meticulous tailor and designer realised Mary and Uffe Frank's dream design with his fine handiwork, so that the dress would fit the bride perfectly.

The bride's tiara was a present from Queen Margrethe and Prince Henrik. The Crown Princess had had a pair of new earrings made for her wedding. The earrings of white gold with diamonds and South Sea pearls were handmade by the jeweller Marianne Dulong.

On the wedding day, Mary carried a beautiful handkerchief, made by the lace-maker and teacher Astrid Hansen. The pattern is a well-known design from Tønder in south-west Jutland named 'The great heart of Denmark'. Astrid Hansen had worked on this six hours a day from the date of the Crown Prince and Princess's engagement on 8 October until Easter in April, when the fine handkerchief was finished. It was the handkerchief that Mary, deeply moved, used to dry her eyes in the cathedral when she heard her mother's favourite hymn, 'Eternal Father'.

Mary

THE WEDDING DINNER AT FREDENSBORG

Menu

Timbale of shellfish from the Nordic Seas
Sea urchin sauce

Spicy roast of venison from the royal forests
Rissolé potatoes from Samsø
Peas Parisienne
Sauté mushroom and morel sauce

Vol-au-vent 'Perfect Union'
(White Danish asparagus and chicken from the island of
Bornholm, perfumed with apple cider)

Cake with white chocolate mousse
'The Crown Prince and Princess'

La Cigaralle du Prince Consort 2000
Cahors Château de Caïx 1996
En Magnum

Champagne Mercier
Cuvée Frederik & Mary

JOHN DONALDSON'S SPEECH ON THE OCCASION
OF THE WEDDING OF THE
CROWN PRINCE AND PRINCESS 14 MAY 2004

Your Majesties, Your Royal Highnesses, honoured guests, family and friends.

In the twelfth century, the marauding Vikings were driven out of Scotland after much savage fighting by a band of men led by the grandfather of the first Donald, the founder of the clan MacDonald. He would have wondered why he went to so much trouble when, some eight centuries later, we take account of today's union between the Viking Frederik and Mary of the MacDonald clan.

For almost four years, my wife, Susan, and I have watched the relationship between Frederik and Mary grow to full bloom, culminating in this magnificent occasion.

Mary made a reluctant entry into the world, but ever since she has eagerly embraced its offerings. Growing up under the combined influences of her mother, Henrietta, and her grandmother, Mary, she has grasped every opportunity to broaden her horizons and has developed into a wonderful woman with many fine attributes.

Memories abound of the bonding between Mary and her mother, the daily tours on the back seat of a bicycle around Clear Lake City, when we lived in Texas; the many early, very early, car journeys down to the first loves of her life, her horses, in Tasmania, and the myriad communications when she moved, after her graduation from the University of Tasmania, to Melbourne. Henrietta would have been so happy for Mary on this her special day.

Min datter er meget smuk. Très belle. Not only, as is obvious, in appearance but in many other ways including how she cares for her family and friends and the manner in which she is approaching the exciting and exacting tasks that lie ahead. I am the proud father of a very loving daughter.

Although fathers these days have little say in such matters, it is with great pleasure and confidence that I entrust her to the care of Frederik: an intelligent, sporting, debonair, delightful young man.

What more could a father-in-law ask? To Frederik: Velkommen to our family. I offer a verse for your reflection from the Scottish national bard, Robert Burns, who says:

To make a happy fireside clime
For little ones and wife
That is the true pathos and sublime
Of human life.

Your Majesties, Your Royal Highnesses, friends.

Please join me in a toast to the bride and groom wishing them a long and happy life together.

Mary showing her 'baby-bump' at Thorshavn, Faeroe Islands, June 2005

Mary attending a fashion show, Copenhagen, June 2005

Mary and Frederik celebrating US President George W. Bush's
59th birthday during his visit to Denmark, July 2005

Commemorative stamp issued in Denmark in honour
of Mary and Frederik's wedding

Frederik's monogram   Mary and Frederik's monogram   Mary's monogram

CROWN PRINCE FREDERIK'S SPEECH TO HIS BRIDE
ON 14 MAY 2004

Your Majesties, Your Royal Highnesses, my dear new family.

Dear John,

What a privilege, what a thrill, what an extraordinary feeling of happiness you have created in me. One might say that Mary also belongs to you – but as of today she belongs to me – and I belong to her.

But there is much more to that sentence than just words. It signifies the end of a period of freedom, of trial and error, where accountability was up to me alone. The sentence also has another side which is only just beginning. To me it means responsibility, trust and sharing.

By allowing me to take Mary's hand and lead her onwards in a new life for better and for worse, you have shown me that you trust me to be capable and responsible in that act throughout life – it's called love. For that I am very grateful to you.

I love her and I will protect her with all my heart. I will do my best to make her feel confident and at home in her new country.

Dear Mary,

In the year 2000 in Sydney, the five Olympic rings were united for the twenty-fifth time. For me, Australia was at that time an unknown and undiscovered continent – symbolised aptly by the fifth and lowest Olympic ring.

I found myself in an unknown country among happy, festive foreigners. My only luggage at that time was my high expectations of my visit, and a certain degree of confidence.

Almost 200 years earlier, another Dane by the name of

Mary

Jørgen Jürgensen had arrived under completely different circumstances, but with just as high hopes and just as much confidence. He left Sydney quite soon after and sailed to Tasmania – your country – one of the states of Australia. Here he managed to create a reputation for himself which ultimately led to his death.

I had only been in Australia two days before our fates were sealed, even though neither of us was aware of it. But your radiance shone clearly for me from our very first meeting. Since then, I have been blinded by it and totally dependent on it.

Until that moment in my life, I had been striving to achieve greater independence, without limiting any of my freedom. My opportunities were plentiful, and my world was often lonely.

But both were continually strengthened in time and in space, because my curiosity and positive faith in the definitive, the ultimate, drove me onwards.

Then you walked into my world and much has already happened. Now, there are two worlds – possibly even more – which from now on we will explore together, side by side. In light and in darkness, in summer, autumn, winter and spring – always.

The joy and strength you give me is like the sun in the daytime which with its radiance melts all doubts and darkness on earth. And like the moon at night, you shine with a watchful and delicate beam of gentleness, which extinguishes the mischief and deceit used by the symbols of darkness.

I often like to compare the dawn's light on a new day to the rebirth of the untouched, the inexperienced and the innocent. A little naïve perhaps – but nevertheless it is wonderful to pretend that everything begins anew. A new world is reborn with the light of a new day.

This moment is 'us' – the two of us – newly together, young together, innocent together, in love together – simply 'together'. You give me security, joy and happiness.

I am almost bubbling over with curiosity as to what the near and distant future has in store for us – and it is you who must answer. But I will try to control myself, for two questions have already been answered with a simple 'Yes' from us both. It is an answer that will hold good for us always. And if we need light in our search for answers, all we need to do is to lift our eyes and look towards heaven. There lies eternity, which can always show us the way back to the path we sometimes lose.

I love you Mary. Come, let us go! Come, let us see! Throughout a thousand worlds, weightless love awaits.

Your Majesties, Your Royal Highnesses,

May I ask you all to rise and join me in drinking a toast to my bride.

Mary

THE BOUNTIFUL PRESENTS

An abundant table of presents bore witness to the thousands of Danes, Greenlanders and Australians who had been generous to the Crown Prince and Princess. In addition to drawings by children, and wine, people had been very innovative and the array of presents revealed that Mary and Frederik's interests cover a wide field and that they are building a bridge between several cultures and continents.

⌒

The present from the people of Denmark, to which thousands of Danes had contributed with small and large donations, was an expensive, hand-painted Flora Danica porcelain dinner set inscribed with the Crown Prince and Princess's monogram. The Danish soul crooner Erann DD composed and recorded a wedding song, 'When you hold me', and the profits from the sales of the CD went to the benefit of disadvantaged children in Greenland via the Association for the Children of Greenland.

⌒

From Greenland, which holds a special place in the heart of the Crown Prince, Mary was given a national costume with a pearl collar and sealskin boots. Two seamstresses from the capital, Nuuk, had worked day and night on the colourful costume, which consists of sealskin trousers and boots and a top made of quilted material covered by silk. The costume is also decorated with lace and a pearl collar. On the same occasion, Frederik received a pair of new boots. The national costume was handed to the Crown

Princess in the summer of 2004 in Nuuk, where Mary paid a visit to Greenland for the first time. The Faeroe Islands presented the couple with similar national costumes.

⟞

The Tasmanian government gave the couple a unique ceramic bowl created by Tasmanian designer Les Blakebrough. Copenhagen University instituted a scholarship for exchange students from the University of Tasmania or another Australian university. According to the stipulations of 'The Crown Princess Mary Scholarship' two scholarships of 10,000 kroner (approx AUD $2000) each will be awarded each year on the couple's wedding anniversary.

⟞

The Australian government gave the couple nine indigenous Australian trees – three each of the Huon pine, snow gum and cider gum – all of which are part of the indigenous flora of Tasmania.

⟞

The present from the Danish government was a genuine Iranian carpet from the mountainous Tabriz region. The hand-knotted artwork is in light, delicate colours and made of wool and silk threads. It measures 24 square metres and consists of more than 17 million knots. It took eight workers two years to create the beautiful carpet.

⟞

Mary

The Danish parliament gave the couple a dining-room table with fourteen China chairs in mahogany, designed by the renowned Danish furniture architect Hans J. Wegner.

⁓

The couple also got horsepower of different varieties. The Crown Princess was presented with a Danish warmblood horse (of a breed well known for its use in competitive equestrian events) from the Association for Danish Warmbloods, and the couple received five cars and a 40-foot yacht, worth millions.

⁓

A painting by the late Australian Aboriginal artist, Jimmy Djelminy, in earth and ochre colours with, among other images, the motif of the rainbow serpent was donated by the Australian–New Zealand Friendship Association in Denmark.

⁓

A stuffed and mounted white Greenland gerfalcon with its prey, a golden plover, was presented to the couple by the Natural History Museum in Aarhus. The birds were framed in a eucalypt case, which was imported from Tasmania.

⁓

The Copenhagen municipality gave Holmegaard glasses for 60 people.

190

The white wine, red wine, dessert wine, water and champagne glasses were all designed especially for the bride and groom by Anja Kjær.

⌣

Aarhus municipality gave the couple the furniture classic 'The Egg', a chair in black leather by the famous architect Arne Jacobsen.

⌣

Fredensborg-Humlebæk municipality, where Mary and Frederik will reside, gave the couple three wickerwork Poul Kjærholm chairs.

⌣

Gråsten municipality joined with other municipalities from South Jutland to give the couple four wrought iron lamps for the avenue leading up to Gråsten castle, where the couple will spend many holidays in the future. When Queen Ingrid celebrated her ninetieth birthday, she had also been presented with wrought iron lamps for the avenue.

⌣

Farsø municipality in North Jutland, where Mary and Frederik often stay at the royal hunting lodge in Trend, gave the couple a fish dish in silver.

⌣

The financial institution Bikubenfonden pleased the couple by instituting a cultural award. Every year, Frederik and Mary will be able to select a Danish artist as recipient of the prize, and with the prize comes a cheque for 500,000 kroner (AUD $100,000). The recipient may be chosen from any branch of cultural life and the prize is presented in connection with a major event of the Copenhagen Opera. The couple will have input into which artists perform at the event and they can also nominate which humanitarian organisation should receive the profits from the ticket sales.

More than 5000 private individuals sent presents to the Crown Prince and Princess on the occasion of the wedding.

MARY'S MONOGRAM

As an engagement present, the Crown Prince and Princess received their own personal joint monogram, and Mary was also given her own personal monogram – which could adorn, among other things, her wedding invitations. In future, anything from place settings and cutlery to porcelain may be personalised by the couple's joint monogram or Mary's own monogram.

Monograms, weapons, coats of arms – all in a modern sense emblems – have been in use since antiquity. Both in ancient Greece and in the Roman Empire, graphic emblems were used on flags, shields and clothing, partly for practical reasons, in order to distinguish friend from enemy, and partly on religious grounds.

In the early Middle Ages, heraldry, which uses coats of arms as identification, was very important, especially for the aristocratic families who were involved in the defence of land. Thus heraldry developed first and foremost among the noble families and royal houses of Europe. Today, heraldry is used not only by royal houses and governments, but also by private enterprise.

The Crown Prince and Princess's joint monogram looks like Crown Prince Frederik's own monogram, which is a so-called mirror monogram, consisting of two F's with their backs to each other. The joint monogrammed F's are placed slightly further from each other than in the Crown Prince's own monogram, because they encircle the letter M, which of course stands for Mary. Above the monogram hovers the royal crown. Queen Margrethe designed the monograms.

Crown Princess Mary was also given her own monogram in connection with the engagement. It consists of a stylised M with a gracious fold in the middle of the letter and with the royal crown above.

The Queen has designed her own monogram, and she is also the originator of Prince Joachim's and Princess Alexandra's monograms.

The Crown Prince and Princess's monograms may be seen on the Crown Prince's home page <www. hkhkronprinsen.dk> while the monograms of the rest of the royal family can be seen on the royal family's home page <www.kongehuset.dk>.

MARY'S FAVOURITE POEM

'How Do I Love Thee'
by Elizabeth Barrett Browning

> *How do I love thee? Let me count the ways.*
> *I love thee to the depth and breadth and height*
> *My soul can reach, when feeling out of sight*
> *For the ends of Being and ideal Grace.*
> *I love thee to the level of every day's*
> *Most quiet need, by sun and candlelight.*
> *I love thee freely, as men strive for Right.*
> *I love thee purely, as they turn from Praise.*
> *I love thee with the passion put to use*
> *In my old griefs, and with my childhood's faith.*
> *I love thee with a love I seemed to lose*
> *With my lost saints, – I love with the breath,*
> *Smiles, tears, of all my life! – and, if God choose,*
> *I shall but love thee better after death.*

(Sonnet XLIII from *Sonnets from the Portuguese*)

Mary

ROYAL SPECIAL DAYS

5 February	Birthday of Crown Princess Mary (born 1972)
16 April	Birthday of Queen Margrethe (born 1940)
29 April	Birthday of Princess Benedikte (born 1944)
14 May	Crown Prince Frederik and Crown Princess Mary's wedding day (married 2004)
26 May	Birthday of Crown Prince Frederik (born 1968)
7 June	Birthday of Prince Joachim (born 1969)
10 June	Queen Margrethe and Prince Henrik's wedding day (married 1967)
11 June	Birthday of Prince Henrik (born 1934)
30 June	Birthday of Princess Alexandra (born 1964)
22 July	Birthday of Prince Felix (born 2002)
28 August	Birthday of Prince Nikolai (born 1999)
30 August	Birthday of Queen Anne-Marie (born 1946)
8 October	Crown Prince Frederik and Mary Donaldson's engagement (engaged 2003)
18 October	Prince Joachim and Princess Alexandra's wedding day (married 1995)

SOURCES

Books

Bistrup, Annelise: *Queen Ingrid*. (Aschehoug) 1997

Danish Queens through a Thousand Years. Editor: Steffen Heiberg. (Gyldendal) 2001

Dich, Preben: *The King of the Dog Days, the story of Jørgen Jürgensen, a Danish adventurer and rebel, who made history on two continents*. (Chr. Erichsen) 1985

Flanagan, Richard: *Gould's Book of Fish*. (Picador) 2001

Freeman, Cathy: *Cathy. Her own story with Scott Gullan*. (Viking/Penguin Books) 2003

Hansen, David: *John Glover and the Colonial Picturesque*. (Tasmanian Museum and Art Gallery and Art Exhibitions Australia) 2003

Høyer, Inge and Henrik Magnild Husum: *Frederik, pictures and reports*. (Høst & Son) 2003

Jørgensen, Poul: *Denmark's Queen*. (Børsens Forlag A/S) 1996

Jørgensen, Poul: *Frederik, Denmark's Crown Prince*. (Møntergården) 1998

Jørgen Jürgensen: King of Iceland, adapted by James Francis Hogan. (Vinten, København) 1973

Journey around Australia. (Politikens forlag/Insight Guides) 2000

Morton, Andrew: *Diana – Her true story*. (Holkenfeldt) 1997

Ninka: *Life's journey. Crown Prince Frederik talks to Ninka*. (Forum) 2002

Ølholm, Torben: *Alexandra. Princess of Denmark*. (Mellemgaard) 2001

Parish, Steve: *Tasmania, Australia*. (Steve Parish Publishing) 2002

Queen Noor: *Leap of Faith. Memoirs of an Unexpected Life*. (Weidenfeld & Nicolson London) 2003

Rubinstein, Mogens: *Queen Margrethe II, 25 years as regent*. (Forlaget Møntergården) 1996

Smitz, Paul: *Tasmania*. (Lonely Planet) 2002

Stilling, Niels Peter: *The Residences of the Royal Family through 1000 years.* (Politikens håndbøger) 2003

Wilkenschildt, Merete: *Royal Weddings in Denmark through 500 years.* (Lindhardt og Ringhof) 2002

Newspapers, TV, internet and research

The Danish Royal Family's home page: <www.kongehuset.dk>

The Crown Prince's home page: <www.hkhkronprinsen.dk>

Denmark Radio's wedding site: <www.dr.dk/bryllup>

TV2: <www.bryllup.tv2.dk>

Norwegian TV, NRK: <www.nrk.no/nyheter/innenriks/kongehuset/ kronprinsbryllupet>

Swedish royal home page: <www.royalcourt.se>

Norwegian royal home page: <www.kongehuset.no>

Belgian royal home page: <www.monarchie.be>

Dutch royal home page: <www.koninklijkhuis.nl>

British royal home page: <www.royal.gov.uk>

The Olympic Movement's official home page: <www.Olympic.org>

Billed-Bladet, years 2001, 2002, 2003, 2004, 2005

Greenland Now

Excerpts from Scandinavian, Australian and English daily newspapers and weekly magazines since September of 2001 including *Aftonbladet*, *BT*, *Berlingske Tidende*, *Dagbladet*, *Ekstra Bladet*, *Journalisten*, *Jyllands-Posten*, *Politiken*, *Se og Hør*, *Sydney Morning Herald*, *The Times*

Crown Princess Máxima, interviewed by Maartje van Weegen and Paul Witteman

DR1's portrait program, *Tracking Mary*, DR1, October 2003

Interview with the Crown Prince and Princess by Andrew Denton, *Enough Rope*. ABC TV, 2005

Excerpt from JJ Film's TV portrait of Mary Donaldson. DR1, May 2004

Research reports from social researcher Mark McCrindle, Mark McCrindle Research Institute, Sydney.

Hello! website: <www.hellomagazine.com>

Citizenship and other legal material via <www.retsinfo.dk> and <www.netjurist.dk>

Official information about Tasmania: <www.tas.gov.au>

The Tasmanian daily newspaper, the *Mercury*, Hobart: <www.themercury.news.com.au>

Earlier issues accessed with the help of the State Library of Tasmania, Hobart.

Factual information about Tasmania: <www.tourismtasmania.com.au>

University of Tasmania: <www.admin.utas.edu.au>

The real estate agent, Belle Property: <www.belleproperty.com.au>

Official information about Australia: <www.australianpolitics.com>

Mary

PICTURE CREDITS

Front cover: Mary at Federation Square, Melbourne, March 2005: Greg Wood/AFP/Getty Images

Back cover: Wedding day, Copenhagen, May 2004: Lars Krabbe/Polfoto

Insert One

Mary attending a gala performance the night before the wedding, Copenhagen, May 2004: Tim Rooke/Rex Features

Five-year-old Mary: Newspix

Henrietta Donaldson: Newspix

Playing hockey for Taroona High School: Tony Palmer/Newspix

Mary and Frederik with Susan and John Donaldson at their home in Sandy Bay, Hobart, January 2004: Jørgen Jessen/Scanpix

Insert Two

Mary at a university reunion, 2001: Scanpix

Mary riding in the grounds of Gråsten Castle, July 2003: Jørgen Kølle/Scanpix

Mary and Frederik's first public kiss, Hobart, January 2003: Jørgen Jessen/Scanpix

Mary and Frederik visiting a museum in Aarhus, April 2004: Claus Fisker/Scanpix

Insert Three

Mary and Frederik's engagement is announced, Copenhagen, October 2003: Steen Brogaard/Colourpress

Susan and John Donaldson, Mary and Frederik, Queen Margrethe and Prince Henrik at the engagement announcement, Copenhagen,

October 2003: Jørgen Jessen/Scanpix

Mary at her first official engagement, Fredensborg castle, October 2003: Jens Noergaard Larsen/Scanpix

Mary and Frederik at Christiansborg palace in the week before their wedding, May 2004: Tim Graham/Getty Images

Insert Four

Frederik sheds a tear as he watches his bride walk down the aisle, Copenhagen, May 2004: Jens Dresling/Polfoto

John Donaldson walks his daughter, Mary, down the aisle, Copenhagen, May 2004: Søren Bidstrup/Scanpix

Mary and Frederik on their wedding day, Copenhagen, May 2004: Lars Krabbe/Polfoto

Mary and Frederik receiving a blessing during their wedding ceremony, Copenhagen, May 2004: Jens Dresling/Polfoto

Insert Five

Mary's first visit to Greenland, June 2004: Keld Navntoft/Scanpix

Mary and Frederik in Greenland, June 2004: Keld Navntoft/Scanpix

Mary and Frederik outside their Fredensborg castle home: Mads Jørgensen/Colourpress

Mary during a Danish lesson: Mads Jørgensen/Colourpress

Insert Six

Mary and Frederik attending Prince Henrik's 70th birthday celebrations, Copenhagen, June 2004: Keld Navntoft/Scanpix

Queen Margrethe, Frederik, Mary and Prince Henrik watch the women's handball at the Athens Olympics, August 2004: AFP

Mary attending a reception at London's Royal Academy of Arts,

September 2004: Dave Benett/Getty Images

Mary at the opening ceremony of Danish parliament, Copenhagen, October 2004: Jørgen Jessen/Scanpix

Insert Seven

Mary on the cover of *Dansk*, February 2005: Scanpix

Mary attending Copenhagen International Fashion Fair, February 2005: Keld Navntoft/Scanpix

Mary and Frederik before racing yachts against each other on Sydney Harbour, February 2005: Mark Baker/AFP/Getty Images

Mary attending Victor Chang Royal Ball with sister Jane, Sydney, March 2005: Ernst van Norde/Scanpix

Insert Eight

Mary attending the 90th anniversary gala dinner for the Australian Red Cross, Sydney, March 2005: Greg Wood/Getty Images

Huge crowds welcomed Mary everywhere on her 2005 Australian tour: Adam Ward/Newspix

Mary and Frederik greeting the crowds outside Sydney Opera House, March 2005: David Gray/Getty Images

Mary visiting patients at Sydney's Westmead Hospital, March 2005: Ernst van Norde/Scanpix

Insert Nine

Mary attending the Danish Lutheran Church in Sydney, March 2005: Greg Wood/AFP/Getty Images

Mary and Frederik with Governor-General Michael Jeffery and Marlena Jeffery at Government House, Canberra, March 2005: Alan Porritt/AFP/Newspix

Frederik trying to make a paper ship at the Nordic pavilion at the World Expo, Nagakute, Japan, April 2005: JIJI Press/AFP/Getty Images

Mary helps to plant a tree at the Hans Christian Andersen park in Funabashi, Japan, April 2005: Toshifumi Kitamura/AFP/Getty Images

Insert Ten

Mary with Thai dancers on her visit to tsunami-affected villages, Khao Lak, Thailand, April 2005: Paula Bronstein/Getty Images

Mary and Frederik during the Hans Christian Andersen bicentenary celebrations, Copenhagen, April 2005: Keld Navntoft/Scanpix

Mary performing her duties as High Patron of Science Day, Helsingor, Denmark, May 2005: Keld Navntoft/Scanpix

Mary and Frederik attending the ballet at the Copenhagen Royal Theatre, June 2005: Martin Høien/All Over Press Denmark

Insert Eleven

Mary showing her 'baby-bump' at Thorshavn, Faeroe Islands, June 2005: Keld Navntoft/Scanpix

Mary attending a fashion show, Copenhagen, June 2005: Kristian Juul Pedersen/Scanpix

Mary and Frederik celebrating US President George W Bush's 59th birthday during his visit to Denmark, July 2005: Martin Høien/All Over Press Denmark

Commemorative stamp issued in Denmark in honour of Mary and Frederik's wedding: AFP/Newspix